W9-CMD-946

"Lynda Ford's ability to get the message across in a 'no-fuss' manner is incredible. Her book is a must read for everyone!"

Cathy Newell, President/CEO,
Mohawk Ltd.

"Lynda's book not only conveys a philosophy for success but more importantly provides the quantitative tools to achieve it. This book should be required reading for any manager at any level."

Donald L. Miller, President/CEO,
Lutheran Care Ministries Network

"These are the problems managers must contend with and Lynda Ford's strategies for overcoming them are exactly what is needed."

Joseph Reinherz, President,
Empire Aero Center,
a subsidiary of Israeli Aircraft
Industries International

TRANSFORM YOUR WORKPLACE

52 PROVEN STRATEGIES TO MOTIVATE, ENERGIZE, AND KICK PRODUCTIVITY UP TO THE NEXT LEVEL

LYNDA FORD

McGraw-Hill

New York   Chicago   San Francisco   Lisbon   London
Madrid   Mexico City   Milan   New Delhi   San Juan
Seoul   Singapore   Sydney   Toronto

1 2 3 4 5 6 7 8 9 0   DOC/DOC   0 9 8 7 6 5

ISBN 0-07-145619-8

McGraw-Hill books are available at special quantity discounts to use
as premiums and sales promotions, or for use in corporate training
programs. For more information, please write to the Director of
Special Sales, Professional Publishing, McGraw-Hill, Two Penn Plaza,
New York, NY 10121-2298. Or contact your local bookstore.

 This book is printed on recycled, acid-free paper containing a
minimum of 50% recycled, de-inked fiber.

Library of Congress Cataloging-in-Publication Data

Ford, Lynda.
    Transform your workplace : 52 proven strategies to motivate,
    energize, and kick productivity up to the next level /
    by Lynda Ford.
        p.   cm.
    Includes index.
    ISBN 0-07-145619-8 (alk. paper)
    1. Employee motivation.   2. Performance.   3. Personnel
management.   I. Title.
HF5549.5.M63F67   2005
658.3'14—dc22   2004029013

Contents

CONTENTS

CONTENTS

Foreword

There are many books on management theory and just as many on quick fix patches that address and redress personnel management issues. But there are few, if any, before *Transform Your Workplace* that take such a broad array of management theories and translate them to best management practices for supervising people. Whether you supervise 1 person, 10, or 1,000, this book has something for you.

Each chapter develops a strategy that can put the supervisor on a fast track to success in managing people. Implementing one such strategy a week for 52 consecutive weeks is indeed a very fast track. But the strategies support one another and serve as building blocks to achieving success . . . for the supervisor, the subordinate, and the organization.

Each strategy is devoted to a single theory and a tool to empower and employ people in the most effective manner to achieve the organization's mission. The strategies stand alone, but taken all together the book provides a powerful and usable instrument for any supervisor to achieve success. Although the book builds a cognitive whole, you can start using the strategies in any order.

A supervisor can start with a chapter that feels right and apply it to the workplace. Indeed, one of the tenets is for you, the supervisor, to make the work environment more interesting (FAST Strategy #27). This enhances confidence (FAST Strategy #46), helps focus on the issue (FAST Strategy #37), and leads to strategies that are usable and solutions that are workable (FAST Strategy #3).

Supervisors and managers may recognize many of these strategies as common sense. But often we all need reinforcement concerning a problem-solving approach or an opportunity to immerse ourselves in a new way of looking at the same issues. One of my favorite chapters concerns the employees' EQ or emotional intelligence quotient (FAST Strategy #26). Fast forward after the introduction and read it. Then you will understand why I urge management at Revere to hire people with a good sense of humor.

At a former company when such a concept was introduced, my group had hundreds of applications from an ad placed in the *Wall Street Journal* and the *New York Times* for a single opening. The list was whittled down to five who were interviewed, of which two appeared outstanding. The one who got the job was able to joke about the process and his prospects! But then, assembling an effective, tight knit team is no laughing matter . . . or is it?

Lynda Ford has worked with our company using this approach with great success. It was a quick and effective way to address a long-term issue. Her FAST 52 approach allowed us to reap almost immediate and sustainable results. The process model and strategies truly work.

So, as you digest this wonderful little book, you'll find some ideas you thought about and some you didn't . . . some things you've tried and some you haven't. The book is rich with nuggets of golden guidelines to make you and your team better supervisors in a better workplace . . . and you will have fun doing it!

M. Brian O'Shaughnessy
Chairman, CEO, and President
Revere Copper Products, Inc.

Acknowledgments

Working on a book is an exhilarating as well as an intimidating process. This was especially the case in writing about a subject that has many intricacies and complexities and bringing it to a level that is pragmatic and understandable with usable strategies. I'd like to first thank my clients, who have taught me much over the years and who have provided valuable opportunities to apply many of the FAST 52 concepts. Each has contributed to my professional growth, and in turn have grown and improved their own workplace environments.

Thanks to my agent, Sandra Bond, and to Melissa Scuereb, my editor at McGraw-Hill, for providing insightful guidance through this process. My colleagues have provided invaluable insight and expertise. Special thanks go to Michael Fain, Michelle Lee, and Milly Valverde for their practical and clear-sighted comments. And thanks to Linda Madore for her resource research.

My thank you list would not be complete without acknowledging two mentors and colleagues. I thank Alan Weiss for giving me sound, to-the-point advice and the guided push I needed (so long ago) in deciding to write this book. Bob Simmen has been an invaluable friend, guide, and sounding board and has been responsible for leading me to the best possible professional decisions.

And last, but certainly not least, is my family, who are always there to support and encourage me. My husband, Greeley Ford; sons Aaron and Daniel Ford; and mother, Helen Myers, have provided me with much support, information, and context. And where would I be without my sisters, Leslie and Bobbie. I thank you from the bottom of my heart for being a part of my life.

Introduction

The idea of FAST 52 originated from countless discussions with managers and employees that revolved around the issue of employee retention. The most common comments were: "We need ideas that we can immediately put to use. We don't have time to do lots of reading, or attend seminars. We need something that can get us started toward improving the work environment. We need ideas that we can implement on our own."

The strategies in *Transform Your Workplace* have been developed based on my own experiences with a variety of organizations. The strategies have not been scientifically tested. They have, however, been used successfully in diverse work settings.

The FAST 52 concept is based on the notion that if you can consider just one idea a week and put many of those 52 ideas to use, you'll see improvements. And, if you have access to just one idea each week, at the end of one year (52 weeks) you'll have laid a solid foundation for an exceptional workplace environment.

The question inevitably arises, "Must I use one idea a week to be successful?" The answer, of course, is no. What's most important is that you work a specific strategy to its logical conclusion. That will often take more than one week. Devoting time each week to specific actions that improve the work environment will allow you to fundamentally change and improve working conditions.

FAST 52 is an acronym that stands for:

Focused—Each FAST 52 strategy is focused on the issue at hand. It is narrowly defined so that you are able to significantly impact the area that you've chosen.

Action-Oriented—The FAST 52 strategy is based on gathering momentum by taking visible actions. There is no room for lip service in FAST 52 management; it is all about taking actions so that employees can see you building a better work environment. These are ideas that are almost entirely within the manager's span of control. For the most part, there is no need to wait for higher levels of approval before implementation.

Simple—Each idea is based on a simple, easy-to-understand premise and is relatively easy to start and to maintain.

Timely—The ideas are timely; that is, they can be used immediately. This allows you to make just-in-time improvements.

52 Weeks a Year—52 ideas, 52 weeks; there's an idea for every week of the year.

The FAST 52 concept allows each strategy to stand alone. So, if FAST Strategy #4 makes more sense for you to start with than FAST Strategy #1, that's okay.

You don't have to go in order unless that's your preference. FAST Strategy #2 is not predicated on successfully completing FAST Strategy #1; jump to the middle or to the end of the book if that's your style.

If you can use all of these strategies, that's great. But chances are you may be using some of them, while you may not be comfortable with others. Pick and choose what works for your organization. If you can implement on a long-term basis even a few of the ideas, you'll realize long-term improvement.

The Retention Connection

Information gathered from exit interviews conducted by our company indicates that employees leave for what we describe as controllable reasons. Controllable reasons are defined as situations that are directly within the company's control to take action and to change. These include areas such as work environment, pay and benefits, relationships with supervisors and coworkers, scheduling, opportunities for advancement, opportunities for training and professional development, ethical issues, job fit, and job duties. Uncontrollable reasons include areas such as relocation of a family member, health problems of either the employee or a family member, return to school, transportation issues, and general personal reasons. In all cases, more than half of the employees left due to controllable reasons.

This points to a company having control over more than half of the turnover problem. In all cases, work environment accounted for the most frequently cited reason why people left the company. Generally, departing employees felt that their opinions and contributions weren't valued and their relationship with coworkers, and especially supervisors, weren't satisfactory. It's no secret that the supervisor or manager is key in setting the tone for a satisfactory work environment, and this data verifies it.

Turnover costs have been estimated at anywhere from 50 to 200 percent of an employee's salary. If that number has you skeptical, then use a very conservative $3,000–$4,000 per employee. The following chart will help you come to that figure:

AREA	COST
Advertising Costs	
Prescreening/Preinterviewing Costs: Reviewing resumes and applications, preparing for interviews, fielding telephone calls, doing administrative paperwork, and performing credential and other background checks	
Interview/Hire Costs: Conducting interviews (1st and 2nd round), reference and other checks, physicals and other exams and screenings, telephone and administrative time, evaluating each candidate, and making the offer (including negotiation time)	
Orientation and Training Costs: Including full orientation period, on-the-job training, and learning curve time (not fully productive)	
Overtime/Contractor Costs: Including other people who must cover the open position	
Other Costs	
Total	

Let's say your company has 300 employees, and your turnover is 20 percent. That equals 60 employees. Take that number times $4,000, and your turnover just cost you $240,000. That's almost a quarter million dollars. Even if just 50 percent of that is due to controllable reasons, you would save $120,000 in that year. That's substantial, and a very conservative estimate.

Loyalty Today

Gone are the days when people receive a gold watch for retiring after 25 years with a company. There is little stability, from both the employee and the employer perspective. The long term has a very different connotation today than it did even a decade ago. When a company does strategic planning, it often means a three-year or perhaps as much as a five-year plan. Ten-year strategic plans are becoming a scarce commodity.

In light of the massive layoffs of 2001, employees are wary about becoming too comfortable with any employer. An employee's perspective turns to gaining as much as possible in the short term, because there may not be a long-term career option with the employer. This causes employees to job-hop, and continually be on the lookout for the next best opportunity. Ten years ago, a resume with four jobs in five years would barely be looked at. Today, it's accepted as commonplace. If we asked employees if they'd like the stability of one employer, given fair pay and benefits and a decent working environment, most would probably say yes. However, this is not their reality.

Employers have turned to layoffs as a short-term strategy for cost cutting, and increasing shareholder value. We call it downsizing, rightsizing, reengineering, and optimum staffing. It is touted as an economic reality, and for these companies, cutting payroll is a matter of survival. Or is it?

What we've lost in all of this is the mutual loyalty between employer and employee. Each side views each other as a commodity, that is, as an object that helps accomplish the task at hand. Somehow the humanness in the employment relationship has been lost, or at least derailed. What the strategies in this book try to do is reestablish the human relationship. It relies on a mutual connection and, with that connection, builds a relationship that is steeped in trust. With that trust comes loyalty.

When we move to a position of mutual trust and loyalty, we find the very qualities that are needed for higher performance levels are right in our workforce. Creativity, innovation, risk taking, problem solving, decision making, leadership, and open communication channels are just some of those qualities. They're right under our collective nose. Our employees have those qualities; they just may not have the right environment to showcase them. As a FAST 52 manager, you'll be able to set that environment on a daily basis.

Here are my "Ten Tips for Becoming a FAST 52 Manager":

1. Recognize that each person is an individual; there is no "one size fits all."

2. Use active listening skills. Frequently check for understanding.

3. Encourage open and honest communication. There may be resistance when you start using some of these strategies. That's natural, and people may be distrustful at first.

4. Set the tone for learning and improvement. Guide your employees and let them act as guides for each other.

5. Make sure your actions are consistent with your values and beliefs. It may sound old or trite, but always walk the talk.

6. If something obviously isn't working, then don't prolong the experience. Go on to something else.

7. Some strategies take longer than others to implement and to show visible results. Think about first implementing strategies that will give you immediate success. You'll be able to build momentum with your group.

8. You'll probably make at least one or two mistakes. Readily admit your shortcomings, and show that you're trying to make things right.

9. Allow a facilitator or trusted colleague to assist you in strategy implementation or offer an outsider's view to help remove roadblocks from the path you're traveling.

10. You know your employees, the work environment, and organization policy and procedures. So tweak the strategies as needed, and use your judgment in deciding how to introduce your group to each strategy.

And now, let the FAST 52 journey begin.

FAST STRATEGY #1

Address Potentially Sticky Situations Head On

A RECENT HEADLINE IN THE LOCAL PAPER read: *"City codes officer suspended for insubordination."* It seems that the codes officer alleged to the newspaper that certain landlords receive preferential treatment from the codes department. When his boss asked him to sit down and explain the problem, the codes officer walked out of the room, precipitating the suspension. The codes officer claimed that the supervisor was well aware of his feelings. Needless to say, that supervisor is probably wishing she had addressed this issue before it hit the newspapers.

Small issue, smaller investment of time rectifying it. Big issue, bigger investment of time rectifying it. It's all about being proactive.

Most of us know that the earlier a sticky situation is addressed, the easier it is to fix. Here are a few tips on how to address potentially sticky situations:

+ If it's in your department, go straight to the source. Don't talk to people who aren't directly involved. Talk to the person(s) involved.

+ Question people in a nonthreatening way, using "I" messages to find out what's going on. Use open-ended questions. Rather than asking, "Is anything wrong?" say, "I sense that something isn't quite right. Let's talk about what might be on your mind." Come to an agreement about how to proceed.

+ If it's a department-wide problem, get everyone's input. If people are reticent about speaking out, arrange for private meetings.

+ If people are reluctant to speak in a group, use some type of checksheet that allows you to gauge the group's mood.

+ If it's outside your department, go to one of your peers (another manager) in the other department. Approach it from the perspective of fixing the *problem*, not the person or people involved. Use a collaborative approach.

Try this formula when there is a potential for conflict or misunderstanding based on a difference of opinion:

+ When I saw (or heard) _____

+ It made me feel _____

✦ For these reasons   _____

✦ And now I'd like   _____

✦ In order to   _____

Using some variation of this formula helps to keep emotions in check without escalating the situation.

FAST STRATEGY #2

Allow Employees to Stretch

REACH FOR THE STARS AND YOU MAY AT least touch the moon. How many of your employees are reaching for the stars . . . or anything? How many are stretching beyond what they think they're capable of accomplishing? To allow employees to stretch, a manager must first identify the competencies that are critical to organizational success, and then identify, in partnership with employees, opportunities to build on those competencies.

For example, if you've identified creativity as an important competency, what types of assignments can you offer employees that will allow them to stretch their creative spirit? Let's take a secretarial position. In what areas could that creativity be sparked? Some areas might be better forms, new ways of handling correspondence, more efficient use of the department calendar, or more customer-focused methods of greeting people who come into your office.

Wherever that creativity is needed, here are a few guidelines to help make that stretch a productive one:

✦ Make sure both parties agree that the project is meaningful and will have impact on the operation.

✦ Provide guidelines to help the employee get started.

✦ Provide the necessary tools and support.

✦ Agree on the deliverable. In this example, the deliverable might be a better process for handling routine correspondence.

✦ Allow the employee some latitude in the means. In other words, unless the employee is straying far from the original intent (the deliverable described above), let the person decide on the best way to get there.

✦ Use frequent checkpoints. It gives the employee opportunity to talk about the project and lets you keep abreast of developments.

✦ Debrief. When the deliverable is complete, review the process. Talk about what went well and what needs improvement. Then, talk about the next "stretch."

✦ Positively reinforce and enthusiastically celebrate the successes. There's always at least one success!

At first you'll find that you must guide employees through the stretching process. But soon, something magical happens. You'll find that employees are taking the initiative to stretch . . . all by themselves! And isn't this what you're working so hard for . . . a self-motivated, high-performance workforce?

FAST STRATEGY #3

Ask for Your Employees' Recommendations on Job-Related Problems

D<small>R. W. E</small>DWARDS D<small>EMING, </small><small>RENOWNED</small> quality expert, urged managers to *"find the problems. It's management's job to work continually on the system."* One of the best ways to find the problems and to work on them is to involve the individuals who are naturally a part of the process.

For example, if you're grappling with how to get better candidates to interview, talk to the people who are closest to the problem. This might include:

+ Employees who work in high-turnover departments. They'll be able to tell you what causes the turnover and what type of person it takes to work there.

+ Employees who work in low-turnover departments. They'll be able to tell you why their department has low turnover and what type of person best fits into that environment.

◆ Employees in your department. What makes them want to stay or to go? What ideas do they have for getting good people through the door.

◆ People responsible for recruiting at your organization.

◆ Internal and external customers.

◆ Supervisors in other departments.

◆ If you're hiring recent college graduates, spend some time in their classrooms to find out what attracts them to an organization. If you're hiring high school graduates, visit the local high school. Teachers love it when businesspeople come in to talk with their students.

◆ If you're hiring professionals, go where they go. Talk to them at professional group meetings and community and social events. Find out what attracts professionals to an organization. But beware: This isn't the time to recruit!

◆ Use focus groups at your organization to discuss specific issues.

◆ Use exit interview data to determine what's good and what's not very good about the organization, and then do something about it!

In a breakfast of bacon and eggs, the chicken is involved but the pig is committed! After you've received input, ask for help in formulating strategies to fix the problem. The more involved employees are, the more committed they'll be to seeing a successful outcome. Involvement is good. Commitment is better!

FAST STRATEGY #4

Assess the Workplace Environment on an Ongoing Basis

Swot. STRENGTHS, WEAKNESSES, OPPORTU-
nities, Threats. In the simplest of terms, a SWOT
analysis is a strategy tool that matches the organization's internal strengths and weaknesses with external
opportunities and threats. It's based on the assump-
tion that a careful review of each component of SWOT
will produce a strategy to ensure organizational success. Generally, what you're doing is identifying the
internal strengths and external opportunities that can
be used to overcome internal weaknesses and external
threats.

Although you can conduct this analysis alone, it's
much better to do it in a group setting. More diverse
people give you a more diverse (and accurate) perspective. Let's see how this might work with a workplace issue:

Issue—*It takes too long to complete the hiring process, from the time an opening is recognized to the day a job offer is extended.*

A SWOT analysis of this issue might begin to take this form:

STRENGTHS	WEAKNESSES	OPPORTUNITIES	THREATS
Staff has a willingness to review issue and is highly motivated to make positive changes.	Work is often uncoordinated— right hand doesn't know what the left hand is doing.	Two local companies recently had large layoffs— additional people in the labor pool.	Tight, competitive job market.
Good relationships with all internal players.	Poor communication.	Have relationship with an outside consultant who can facilitate the process.	Not attracting high-caliber candidates.
All involved are excellent interviewers.	The hiring process has a number of steps viewed as unnecessary.	Outside community views the organization as "world class."	Candidates tell us that they are kept hanging for too long before an offer is made.

As you continue on with the SWOT analysis, you can begin to see how your strengths might be used to overcome your weaknesses and how you can turn those threats into opportunities. One great strength is that the staff has a willingness to review and to make changes. This can go a long way in improving the coordination of work and communication systems.

The fact that there are good internal relationships and that the community perceives the organization as world class can be used to leverage publicity about the positive work environment, which in turn may be pivotal in being successful in a tight job market.

FAST STRATEGY #5

Be a Management Gladiator

I F YOU HAVEN'T SEEN THE MOVIE *GLADIATOR*, I highly recommend renting it for a day or two. The lead character, Maximus, is a Roman general, turned slave, turned gladiator, turned savior of Rome. As general for Caesar's legion, Maximus had the respect and admiration of his followers. As a gladiator, fighting in the arenas that dotted the countryside and finally at the Roman Colesseum, he had the respect and admiration of his fellow gladiators and the crowd. Why? Because he embodied the truest and most basic qualities that people look for in their leaders:

✦ Willingness to lead the task at hand and then work side by side. Maximus did not expect his followers to do anything that he would not do himself. In fact, he took the lead and set the tone. Whether it was fighting Germania or

Commodus the Emperor of Rome, he led by example. And he continued to stand next to his men, encouraging them, protecting them, and celebrating their successes.

+ Balance. While Maximus's accomplishments as a general and a gladiator would have been plenty, we are constantly reminded of his devotion to his wife, son, gods, and country. Maximus worked to keep an enviable balance in his life.

+ Integrity. All of his decisions were steeped in "doing the right thing." He approached each challenge in his life without self-interest or self-reward.

+ Focus on the bigger picture. All that Maximus did was based on his belief of a better Rome. Each action that he took, including his death, was done to achieve the long-term goal . . . returning Rome to the control of the Senate.

How can you use these four qualities to improve your leadership? Would your employees see these qualities in you? Are you a management gladiator?

FAST Strategy #6

Be Available

"**W**E'RE PROUD OF THE FACT THAT OUR company practices an open-door policy!" In a recent exit interview, an ex-employee stated, "My manager says that he has an open-door policy, but it's really not true. He thinks an open-door policy is all about seeing us when it's convenient for him, but he's only here two days a week. There are lots of problems that come up when he's not here, and we can't ever find him to discuss them. If we try to handle it on our own, we get disciplined. It's a no-win situation, and that's mostly why I left. If he had made himself more available, maybe I would have stayed."

Available means not only having your door open, but also being visible at the worksite. This might mean having face-to-face conversations, either formally or informally. In this day and age of virtual teams and people who are spread from site to site, sometimes that isn't so easy. You can also be visible to your employees through:

✦ Casual telephone conversations

✦ E-mail

✦ Forwarding information, such as memos, articles, and other news items of importance

Let's spend a minute talking about the do's and don'ts for effectively using the above mechanisms.

Phone or E-mail Do's and Don'ts

Do casually call or e-mail to:

✦ See how it's going

✦ Ask for more details on an ongoing project

✦ Positively reinforce good performance

✦ Ask what you can do to help make employees' jobs easier

✦ Brief employees on new developments in the department or the company

✦ Check on certain milestones, i.e., project completion

✦ Touch base before or after vacations, weekends, etc.

Don't casually call or e-mail to:

✦ Discipline or otherwise chastise an employee for a less than stellar performance

✦ Blow off steam about anything

✦ Be perfunctory or look or sound like you are

✦ Use language that isn't 100 percent acceptable (cursing never is)

Forwarding Information Do's and Don'ts

Do forward information to:

✦ Keep employees in the loop

✦ Present employess with new information that will be useful to their work

✦ Validate what employees are currently working on

Don't forward information that:

✦ Shows employees they're doing something incorrectly

✦ Is self-serving and validates your point of view

✦ Is of no value to employees

Inevitably, the question of how to handle sticky situations by phone comes up. Can these be handled by phone? Sometimes that's the only option. When this is the case, schedule time with the employee; don't catch him or her off guard. Let the employee know what you want to talk about in advance so that he or she, too, can prepare for the conversation. Then, when the conversation is over, send the employee a written account so that both of you are on the same sheet of music. Back to FAST Strategy #1—Address Potentially Sticky Situations Head On.

FAST STRATEGY #7

Infuse Passion and Let It Show

*One person with passion is better than
forty people merely interested.*
—E. M. Forster (1879–1970)

A FTER I HAD FINISHED A CONFERENCE KEY-
note presentation, my host greeted me at the side of the
stage with a smile and said, "It's evident how passionate you are about the human resources profession.
As professionals, we try to stay even keeled, but it's so
important to have that fiery passion so we can lead
others." When I asked my host what she meant by passion, she said, "It's conviction. It's enthusiasm. But even
more than that, it's evident how much you love what
you do and the possibilities that your work offers."

That started a conversation about how passion is
missing in the workplace, particularly among managers. We have been programmed to keep ourselves
under control, not to get too emotional. This is a liti-
gious society, and we must take appropriate actions to
minimize potential liability for our companies. Unfortunately, we've lost an important leadership quality.

Passion is often likened to loud, overbearing emotion, a sexual connotation, or even suffering. In busi-

ness, we might think of a person forcefully raising his or her voice or wildly gesticulating. In this case, passion means enthusiasm without limits, or a deep, burning devotion to something or someone.

Passion can often be the difference between good and great, between mediocrity and achievement. It can be the difference in what helps you lead your employees to greater levels of performance. Ask yourself these questions:

- ✦ Do I love my job? If not, do I at least *really* like it? (It's okay not to love or really like fill-in jobs during your early years, but when you're in a position of leading and managing others, this is critical.)

- ✦ Am I enthusiastic? How do I show it?

- ✦ How would other people describe my attitude toward my job?

If your answers point to anything less than a high level of enthusiasm and excitement, it might be time for a tune-up. Every job has its fair share of mundane tasks, problems, and obstacles, but the best managers don't focus on those. The focus is on what they love about the job, what they are passionate about. And that focus translates into a better work environment.

When the going gets tough, think about what brought you to that job in the first place. Where was your initial passion? How did that job-related passion grow? How can you stoke the fires of passion to get back on track (and yes, I think this works for relationships, too . . . although that's another book!)?

FAST Strategy #8

Be Positively Unpredictable When It Counts

Same old, same old . . . or is it? As managers, we are drilled in consistency, in treating people fairly, and in having predictable responses. There's good reason for that. In any organization, employees need to know that when certain events transpire, there will be predictable responses. We even teach managers how to do this in classes on behavior modification. It helps to promote an environment where employees can feel a certain degree of physical and emotional security. To some extent, that's the way it should be. Or should it?

Sometimes unpredictability, properly placed, can have tremendous impact on morale. I'm not talking about unpredictably chastising employees or unpredictably not showing up for a scheduled meeting. Good manners and proper etiquette must always prevail. The type of unpredictability I'm talking about has more to do with camaraderie and positive influence.

Try some of these suggestions:

✦ If you're the one who never makes the coffee, then learn to make it!

✦ If you're the one who rarely has time for lunch, then bring pizza in for everyone!

✦ If you're the one who takes phone calls during meetings, then put on the DND (do not disturb)!

✦ If you're the one who waits for employees to come to you for help or advice, then seek them out *before* they come to you!

✦ If you're the one who always stays late, then leave on time (and insist that your staff leave, too)!

You get the idea . . . the point is that this unpredictability can be like a breath of fresh air and energize your workforce. Employees certainly notice when you do something out of character, and when it's positive it can have a ripple effect throughout your organization. Employees will often follow your lead, so just a few randomly placed acts of unpredictability can light a flame of enthusiasm and newfound morale.

FAST STRATEGY #9

Build Positive Alliances, Even with the Not-So-Positive

IT'S EASY TO WORK WITH THE PLEASANT people. It's easy to build relationships and alliances with those who share similar points of view or who are just nicer to work with. But then there's the other side . . . the people with whom we must work, but don't like to.

Often our first inclination is to either put up barriers or try to ignore people whom we find difficult. Why do we need more difficult people in our lives? However, there is good to be gained by building these alliances. As a supervisor, you can demonstrate the power of building positive alliances and reap the benefits.

+ Look at those who play an integral part in the operation of your department but who are perceived as difficult. What are their strengths? What can you do to capitalize on those strengths?

✦ Whom can you enlist to help you build alliances? Find the people everyone likes and talk with them. They'll probably be glad to offer you some insight into their relationship success.

How do you go about implementing just one of their insights? Here's an example close to home. At the beginning of my human resource career, I had a boss about whom I felt mostly ambivalent. One day, though, he got my attention, and it was at that point I realized the power he had in building positive alliances.

The company accounting system was undergoing a major change—everything was to be automated. To most people that was a welcome change. After all, keeping manual records was cumbersome and not always accurate. However, the accounting supervisor had a different perspective. She was not at all happy about the impending change and was doing all she could to fight it. She visited my boss regularly to complain about everything that would go wrong with the new system. The complaining was no surprise— the accounting supervisor had a reputation as a "professional complainer." Most of us just wrote her off as not being a team player.

My boss listened to her, and then he said, "It sounds like you have some real concerns. Could you write all of them down for me and get that to me by the end of the week?" What could she say? By the end of the week, my boss had five handwritten (front and back) pages of everything that could possibly go wrong during the conversion. He then went to see the MIS director, handed him a copy of the list and said, "Here's everything that Mary thinks could go wrong. I'd like for both of you to meet to talk about it and see if these items can be addressed."

Fast forward to the end of the story. After several meetings, all of the items had been addressed. The conversion occurred on time. And, it was smooth sailing! You see, my boss capitalized on Mary's strength—her ability to complain! He used that in a way that built a positive alliance. The conversion went off without a hitch, Mary was part of the process, and there were no casualties along the way.

FAST Strategy #10

Celebrate the Small Stuff

ACCORDING TO *THE AMERICAN HERITAGE Dictionary of the English Language, celebrate* is defined as, "To observe (a day or event) with ceremonies of respect, festivity, or rejoicing; to perform (a religious ceremony); to extol or praise; to make widely known; display; to engage in festivities."

We all know what it's like to "engage in festivities." We engage in festivities when we celebrate employee anniversaries and birthdays, successfully completed projects, and individual and team achievements. We display our pride on "Walls of Fame" that feature employees of the month and other organizational achievers. Senior leadership may frequently extol or praise employees from the podium at an organization-wide meeting.

That covers the big stuff, but what about the smaller, everyday stuff? Here's where "ceremonies of respect" come into play.

Usually when we think about ceremonies of respect, we immediately think of religious ceremonies, swearing-in ceremonies, or something similar. Again, this is the big stuff. There are opportunities every day for you to fashion your own personal ceremonies of respect, and use them to reinforce the daily small stuff that so often slips through the cracks. Here are a few suggestions to get you started on developing and maintaining your own ceremonies of respect:

✦ Look for something that will be the "tie that binds" with your employees. For example, could you have a weekly or monthly lunch for no other reason than to say, "Thank you for being here every day." Be sensitive to employee needs and desires. Just a note—celebrating a weekly lunch with pizza is fine, but not if someone is lactose intolerant! Be aware of dietary restrictions.

✦ Involve your employees in developing rituals and traditions. You might be surprised with their ideas, especially the simplicity of them. For example, one secretary, given the opportunity to fashion a ritual, decided that a 10-minute cup of coffee with her boss each morning was important to her. The intent? It was nothing more than to get the day off to a good start and to build the personal relationship. The time he took with her said, "I respect you enough and think you're important enough to spend time with you (*and I won't ask you to type a memo!*)." No cost, but a big payout.

◆ Keep it up! Nothing screams fad of the month more loudly than a good intention that gets swept under the carpet. It's up to you to ensure that these small celebrations become an integral part of your work environment.

FAST Strategy #11

Delegate, Enrich, and Empower

"THE PEOPLE'S CAPACITY TO ACHIEVE IS determined by their leader's ability to empower" states John Maxwell in *The 21 Irrefutable Laws of Leadership*. Good leaders figure out how to delegate meaningful tasks to enrich an employee's job. Enrichment does not mean enlargement. And indiscriminate "task dumping" is just that—job enlargement. Good managers are deliberate and think carefully before delegating. Strong leaders take this one step further and empower employees to achieve their goals. This is not an easy task. Too often, for fear of project or personal failure, leaders meddle with the means and undercut employees in their quest for empowerment.

> *It would take so long to teach someone,*
> *that I might as well do it myself.*

There is some truth to that statement. In our busy environments, we have a tendency to focus on what needs to be done immediately. What usually needs to be done NOW can be most quickly accomplished by doing it ourselves. However, as supervisors, not only are we responsible for getting the work done, but we are responsible for developing the people who report to us. Delegation is one of the ways we develop staff skills and lay the foundation for an empowered workforce.

Delegation serves several purposes:

✦ It helps you to better manage not only your time, but the time of those people who report to you.

✦ It provides learning opportunities, which lead to empowered employees.

✦ It allows you to reallocate work so that you can focus on the most important areas.

Here are my "Six Tips for Effective Delegation":

1. Identify what work can be delegated. If you have identified something that cannot be delegated, ask yourself why.

2. Be familiar with the background, skills, credentials, and capabilities of the person who will be performing the delegated work.

3. Make sure that you are available (especially in the beginning) to answer questions. If there are opportunities for the person to make independent decisions, let him or her know. If you will not be available, have another person act as your backup.

4. Be clear in your communications. How does the person best relate to information? Be prepared to present instructions using a variety of methods. Use active listening skills to check for understanding.

5. Establish process checks or checkpoints to review progress.

6. Give constructive feedback to modify or continue performance.

FAST STRATEGY #12

Encourage Community Involvement, Tap into the Energy

Iᶠ ʏᴏᴜ ᴡᴀɴᴛ ᴛᴏ ꜰɪɴᴅ ᴏᴜᴛ ᴡʜᴇʀᴇ ʏᴏᴜʀ employees' enthusiasm and true talents lie, just look at what they do outside of work. Every community benefits from the volunteers who give their time, energy, and money to a vast array of nonprofit agencies, religious groups, and youth activities. They are coaches; participants in walk-a-thons, marathons, and telethons; tutors; envelope stuffers; board members; book readers; clean-up crews; and house builders. The list goes on and on. While the activities are as diverse as the people themselves, they all have one thing in common: Giving their talents for a greater good.

How do you harness that enthusiasm
and talent in the workplace?

Generally, people give of themselves outside the workplace because they get some intrinsic level of satisfaction. It taps into one or more of their "Engines of Motivation." Some of those engines are: Engine of Ownership, Engine of Significance, Engine of Belonging, Engine of Recognition, Engine of Achievement, Engine of Power and Authority, and Engine of Competency (based on Dean Spitzer's *Supermotivation,* Amacon, 1995). We are all driven to some degree by one, and sometimes several, of these engines.

The trick, of course, is to find out which engine(s) is driving which person. Although motivation is a very individual thing, here's what you can immediately do:

+ Ask employees if they're involved in outside activities, and if so, which ones.

+ Ask employees why they're involved and what they get out of their activities.

+ Ask them what special skills or talents they use during the community activities that they're not able to use on the job.

+ Ask if they would like to be able to use more of those talents on the job.

+ Ask if they would like to work together to develop a plan to utilize more of the talents they've described.

FAST STRATEGY #13

Es, Es (or Eat, Eat)

FOOD PROVIDES A POWERFUL BOND, AND IN many cultures food is inextricably linked to sharing events. Weddings, funerals, birthdays, retirements, religious services, and even the Super Bowl are events that are built around food. Food is associated with fellowship and sharing. It not only feeds our bodies, it also fuels our souls. Events and rituals built around food and work can also improve the workplace environment.

One company I know uses food as a means of furthering its commitment and understanding of diversity issues. Each week features a specific type of lunch. For example, this week might be Mexican, next week Japanese, the week after Jamaican, the next week Native American, and so forth, until each culture represented in the company has been highlighted. Food is either purchased or brought in by employees. After everyone has been served, a brief program is conducted that highlights that particular culture. It might be a video, a lecture, a discussion, or a skit. The point is, people have an opportunity to enjoy good food and fellowship, and learn something that is important to their organization's culture.

Another company I know sponsors a "Lunch and Learn" session each month. Pizza or sandwiches are available at no charge to employees. While eating, a professional development topic is presented that is of interest to the group. It might be on communications, presentation skills, or how to better manage conflict. The lunch gives people an opportunity to meet and learn in a relaxed environment.

A supervisor at a third company was working under a tight deadline to get a mailing out. She told her secretary to hold all her calls and that she was not to be disturbed because the mailing had to be finalized. It looked like an extraordinarily long night. After a few minutes, her secretary knocked on the door. She said that she had talked to everyone in the department, and all but one would stay late to help get the mailing out. As it was, everyone was at the office until about 8:00 p.m. About 5:00 p.m., the supervisor made a call and had pizzas brought in. This proved to be the proverbial icing on the cake. Working and eating, the job got done in a congenial, warm atmosphere.

Look for opportunities. How can you use food to help improve your work environment? Not sure? Ask your employees! They will most certainly give you suggestions that can be used immediately!

FAST STRATEGY #14

Find Opportunities to Collaborate with Other Departments, Units, Etc.

IN A RECENT SURVEY AT A LARGE COMPANY, employees rated relationships in their own teams or departments as very positive. However, when it came to relationships with other departments, the rating was downright negative. Additionally, the employees who were surveyed felt that these negative relationships were preventing them from doing the best job possible. When asked what was being done to improve the situation, not one person could identify a single, tangible action.

The truth is, most of us do not operate in a vacuum. No person is an island, and that goes double for departments and work teams. We not only rely on people in our own departments, but often we must share critical information with people in other departments, divisions, worksites, and even outside the organization. Too busy to forge relationships with everyone? Try this process to get started:

1. Identify the critical work processes that your department must perform (remember to involve everyone in the department).

2. Identify which functions go outside of your department.

   ✦ What information is passed on by your department?

   ✦ What information is received by your department?

3. What is the relationship with the department on the giving/receiving end? (Use a 1–5 rating— 1 meaning the relationship is abysmal, 5 meaning the relationship is terrific.)

4. For all those receiving a 1, 2, or 3, prioritize how important that department is in your work processes.

5. Develop an action plan, one department or person at a time. For example, in one company, the human resources (HR) department must often interface with the finance department. The HR department rated the relationships with accounts payable and payroll as a 2. The action plan looked something like this:

STEP NUMBER	ACTION	PEOPLE RESPONSIBLE	DONE BY
1	Department heads meet to discuss the situation, develop a schedule, and agree on outcomes and goals.	HR Director/ Controller	April 1
2	Meeting is scheduled to discuss concerns and how the work relationships can be improved. All departments are separately briefed so that everyone has the same understanding.	HR Director/ Controller responsible for arranging for people in applicable departments to be present	April 15
3	Meeting occurs. At the meeting specific actionable items are agreed on, including an evaluation mechanism.	Department employees, with oversight from management	April 22
4	Follow up occurs to ensure that all actionable items are occurring.	Department employees, with oversight from management	Through June 1
5	Assess progress on goals (evaluation mechanism) to assess improvement.	Department employees, with oversight from management	June 7
6	Meet again to review progress.	Department employees, with oversight from management	June 10

FAST Strategy #15

Find Out What Motivates Employees, and Then Use It

ONE OF THE MOST COMMON MANAGEMENT complaints I receive is, "I just can't find people who are motivated. They sometimes start that way, but in a few months, all the enthusiasm and motivation for the job has disappeared." While working with Jim, a manager in a professional services firm, we looked at exactly this issue.

Jim said he used a variety of techniques to try to keep the motivation level high. He used lots of "atta boys," certificates, time off, pizza parties, and even money to keep people motivated. Unfortunately, for all of Jim's good intentions, he wasn't motivating anyone. He was making a common mistake: tapping into the wrong motivation engine.

Jim eventually sat down with each person in his group and asked what he or she wanted to get out of the job. He probed deeper to learn what each person found meaningful in the job. With the five people who reported to him, he got four different answers.

One person said that she wanted her special skills to make a difference in the services that the company offered. Two others said their job was most meaningful when they had a significant role in deciding how the work was done. And one person liked the social aspect of the job as much as the job itself. Armed with this new information, Jim was ready to tap into each person's motivation engine and start revving up his work group.

Consider these motivation engines (based on Dean Spitzer's *Supermotivation*, Amacon, 1995):

Engine of Ownership

People have an innate desire to possess tangible (and intangible) goods. Very often, we measure our self-worth by what we own, such as our home, vehicle, clothing, or jewelry. We take pride in those things that we consider to be ours. The same is true with intangibles, such as values and ideas. Think about how you felt the last time someone disagreed with you or criticized a closely held belief. Employees have the same desire to own their jobs—materials, ideals, and the work they produce.

Engine of Significance

We want what we do to be deemed important. We want our contributions to be meaningful and to make a difference. We want to have an impact on those who are important to us. We want our endeavors to be worthy. This is often done through charity work, or through social or religious causes. Imagine if that energy could be unleashed at the workplace. As supervisors and as managers, we need to find outlets at work to help our employees find their work meaningful and significant.

Engine of Belonging

Human beings are social by nature and want to belong to a group. This is seen at college campuses with fraternities and sororities, community service organizations like Rotary and Kiwanis, and groups like the Shriners. We see numerous groups at senior centers, bowling leagues, and professionally oriented groups. The workplace provides critical contact and opportunities for socializing and relationship building. In fact, for some, work is *the* social cornerstone.

Engine of Recognition and Achievement

Nothing succeeds like success! Achievement is a measure of success and breeds even more achievement. People innately like to meet and exceed goals in the workplace. Achievement is usually the product of hard work, determination, and/or perseverance. The very fact that someone has achieved something brings a feeling of pride and accomplishment from within. However, it's also important that others, particularly supervisors in the workplace, recognize those accomplishments. All of us want to be sincerely appreciated for the contributions we make.

Engine of Power and Authority

Although the desire for power and authority is rooted in human nature, when given the opportunity to obtain it, we often turn the other way. *Empowerment* is a term we hear today, yet employees often act as if they do not want to be empowered. We naturally resist external control (remember rebellious teenagers), yet when given the opportunity to exercise control, we are reticent to take it. Why? Organizational structure. The organization very much dictates what we can and cannot do. There are policies and procedures and guidelines and regulations that can sap any feelings of power and authority. Managers must ensure that the infrastructure reinforces empowered employees rather than taking away control.

Engine of Competency

Virtually all human beings want to feel as if they are good at something. We want to skillfully master tasks through self-learning and learning from others. It is by gaining competence that we develop self-esteem—the feeling that we are truly capable and skillful.

How can you tap into one or more of these engines to help spark motivation in your workforce?

FAST Strategy #16

Give Credit

IN THE EARLY YEARS OF MY CAREER, I WAS PUT in charge of pharmacy recruiting for a retail drugstore chain. The company was growing, with a dozen more stores on the planning board, all requiring two pharmacists each. The only problem was the severe shortage of pharmacists. Out of 91 possible pharmacist openings, we were down 27, nearly one-third. Aside from the fact that we had severe staffing problems, we couldn't even open the new stores unless we had pharmacists to assign to those stores.

Digging into the problem with a vengeance, I quickly found three main issues that were keeping us from hiring and holding on to pharmacists. The first was that our competition was paying a small amount more, but just enough to make the newer pharmacists jump ship. The second was a perceptual issue. In the recent past, our company had required pharmacists to take preemployment polygraph examinations. Many refused. We dropped the requirement, but there was still a perception in the pharmacy community that the polygraph was a requirement. The last issue had to do with college relations. We would go to the pharmacy college on interview day only to have a handful of the 60 possible graduates on our schedule. The students just didn't see us as a viable career option.

To solve these problems, I convinced senior management to raise salaries (we were losing it in overtime anyway). Then came my one-woman public relations campaign. I went into every drugstore I saw and talked about opportunities at the company and how we no longer had a polygraph requirement. Then came college relations. By building and maintaining relationships with the faculty and administration, who became our greatest cheerleaders, we went from a handful of interviews to nearly 50. The result? We went from 27 vacancies, plus 12 new pharmacists needed, to filling almost all positions.

Basking in the success, I happened to overhear the director of my department say that he was responsible for the program success. At a meeting later that week, kudos were given to my director for allowing the company to move forward and continue to grow. As I looked at my director, he looked away and never addressed the issue. Needless to say, that was the last time I put that type of time and energy into solving an organizational problem. It killed off my dedication and loyalty to the company. All it would have taken was for my director to say, "I think we need to thank Lynda for her efforts in this project."

Where are the opportunities for you to set aside your own desire for recognition to ensure that your employees receive it? Take a look at these opportunities:

✦ At meetings

✦ At breaks

✦ At lunch

✦ While talking to a third party

✦ During informal performance reviews

✦ Formally—on a bulletin board, at a formal recognition program, or at a similar event

✦ In an article, memo, or other written piece

✦ On camera

✦ Off the record

Giving credit where credit is due returns dedicated, loyal employees.

FAST STRATEGY #17

Use SIMPLE Feedback

Feedback is the breakfast of champions!
—Rick Tate

THERE'S NOTHING LIKE CONSTRUCTIVE FEED-
back for improving and changing employee performance. For organizations looking for a big return on
investment, well, look no further. This is it! Feedback
costs nothing. Anyone can give and receive it at
almost any time. And, done correctly, it has far-
reaching and long-lasting results.

For feedback to be truly effective, keep it SIMPLE:

- ✦ **S**ensitive

- ✦ **I**ssue Related

- ✦ **M**eaningful

- ✦ **P**rompt

- ✦ **L**isten

- ✦ **E**asy to Understand

Sensitive

Start establishing relationships by respecting people's sensitivities. When giving feedback, this means being aware of the issues and buttons that help and hinder effective feedback. For example, if the person who you're giving feedback to is hypersensitive or overly emotional, consider saving the discussion for the end of the day, and preferably on a Friday. That way, the person has an opportunity to think about what's been discussed, and if it's less than favorable, there is opportunity to regain one's composure and not have to face an office full of inquiring minds. Also, think about the different sensitivities that come from diverse cultural backgrounds. There are also different perceptions based on age, gender, ethnic and religious background, sexual orientation, and race. Consider those factors when giving feedback.

Issue Related

If you're looking to give feedback on a specific subject, make sure that it's just that . . . specific! Keep it relevant to the issue at hand and don't load on other stuff. If you want the person to focus, then it's important for you to focus, too. Resist the urge to cover just one more thing.

Meaningful

Can the person take action on the feedback you're giving? For example, an employee may have a problem getting to work on time. If the feedback is designed to reaffirm the company's attendance policy and get the employee's commitment to be on time, you may be missing the mark. If the root of the problem is that the school bus comes late each morning and the employee cannot leave until the school bus has picked up her first-grader, then the feedback needs to be designed to address the issue at hand—the school bus schedule and how the work schedule might be flexed. Getting feedback on areas where you can exercise little or no control only leads to frustration.

Prompt

Feedback is best given shortly after the event that triggers the need for feedback. If the employee has done something well, don't wait until the quarterly review to mention it; likewise if performance problems need correction. Frequent, sincere, and applicable feedback helps to promote an environment of open and honest communication. There's no time like the present! And, remember to use feedback for the positive as well as the developmental areas.

Listen

Although by the very act of giving feedback you're the one speaking, you can make feedback more effective by making it two-way. Use active listening skills, both attending and reflecting. Be aware of body language and use repetition and paraphrasing. Check for understanding, and let the person who you're talking with know that you really understand the core of his or her message.

Easy to Understand

Use words, analogies, and examples that are easily understood. Be careful of jargon or slang. If the person has a different cultural background, be aware of language that might be misinterpreted. Use neuro-linguistic programming (NLP) to help others take in and process information more effectively. If the person is more visual (processes information best by seeing), write things down, or use pictures or flip charts. If the person is more auditory (processes information best by hearing), make sure that there is a lot of two-way discussion. If the person is kinesthetic (processes information best by doing), think about using role-plays or games to emphasize a point.

FAST STRATEGY #18

What I Like About You

Fᴿᴏᴍ ᴛɪᴍᴇ ᴛᴏ ᴛɪᴍᴇ, ᴡʜᴇɴ I'ᴍ ᴡᴏʀᴋɪɴɢ with a group over a multiple-day period, tensions can mount and emotions run high, especially if the group is in unfamiliar territory. Although groups do come together and make progress, it's sometimes difficult to remember that there was once enjoyment in working together. To bring a group or team together, and to reinforce the positive, I lead the group through the following exercise:

1. Each person receives as many sheets of paper as there are people in the group.

2. Envelopes are placed on a separate table with each person's name on an envelope (one envelope per person).

3. The back of each person's chair is labeled with his or her name.

4. I then ask each person to think about the best qualities of each person. Each person chooses three best qualities.

5. Each member of the group then uses a separate sheet of paper for each person, puts the name on top, and writes down those three best qualities. (This is where the labeled chairs come in handy . . . not everyone remembers everyone's name.)

6. No one signs his or her name; this is an anonymous exercise.

7. At the completion of the exercise, all slips are handed to me and I place them into each person's envelope. (I do read the notes before placing them in the envelope to ensure that the spirit of the exercise is carried out properly.)

8. I then seal the envelopes, and at the end of the session, I distribute them to the participants.

As you might expect, the participants race to their cars to tear open the envelopes. It's not unusual for one or two to come back into the room, or to call me in a few days and say thank you for a great send-off. How can you adapt this to send off your team on a positive note?

FAST STRATEGY #19

Involve Employees in Decision Making Whenever Possible

D URING EXIT INTERVIEWS, AN INTERESTING
piece of information that often comes out is that
employees do not feel their input is considered in
decision making. It's not unusual to hear employees
say that although they have the authority to make
small decisions to get their jobs done, when it comes
to decisions that have a major impact on their work
lives, they aren't asked for input. Furthermore, they
also state that they do not understand the reasoning
behind many of the decisions that are made.

Think about it. Here's an opportunity to build relationships and to enhance the level of employee commitment. It doesn't cost anything. A person with a
hand in the design phase is much more likely to be
committed to seeing it through to a successful outcome. If you want to build a committed workforce, it

would stand to reason that you'd ask for employee input and then act on that input whenever possible.

You may say that it's too time-consuming; there are other, more important things you must work on. Could one of those more important things be hiring new staff? What a waste! Here's a way to get started:

1. Sit down and make a list of the most important decisions that need to be made in your department (or business unit, division, etc.).

2. Look at the staff you have and decide in which areas they could have the most positive impact. In the beginning, go for the quick win.

3. Call your group together:

    ✦ Explain that you'd like their input on whatever area you've chosen.

    ✦ Give them whatever background information they'll need.

    ✦ Specifically state what you want as the outcome or goal. Quantify. (We need to reduce processing time by seven days.)

    ✦ Outline any parameters. (Can't cost more than x, must be stand-alone, etc.)

    ✦ Make the resources they'll need available to them. (Time, money, materials, etc.)

    ✦ Give the group a general time frame, but let them develop the time line.

4. Answer any questions they have and be prepared to offer assistance whenever needed.

It is important for you to commit to using the group's suggestions. If you are effectively facilitating the group, what they come up with shouldn't surprise you. Although this process may be a bit more time-consuming in the beginning, the payback is tenfold. You're building a self-sufficient, self-directed team. That's a powerful force in an exceptional work environment.

FAST STRATEGY #20

Involve Employees in the Hiring Process

W HEN I'M LOOKING TO HIRE MORE PEOPLE and I have a high-performing person working with me, the first thing I ask is, "Anymore like you?" Chances are, the people they recommend have the same great work ethic. I also ask people who work with me to get involved in the process. It might involve assessing a resume, sitting with someone and conducting a realistic job preview, or participating in the interview. There are many opportunities for involvement.

Here are my "Top Ten Ways to Involve Employees in the Hiring Process":

1. Have employees determine the behaviors that are needed to perform the job (that you're hiring for) successfully. Employees can gather firsthand information and ask other job incumbents and managers. The output of this is a list

of 5 to 10 characteristics a person needs in order to be successful in that job.

2. Involve employees in writing the interview questions based on the characteristics identified in #1.

3. Involve employees in the actual interview process, with a defined, substantive role. This means actively participating, not just observing.

4. Delegate writing the interview summaries and any scoring that might go along with the summaries. For example, you may score applicants on the way they answer each behavior-based question.

5. Establish criteria for prescreening resumes or applications, and then let the employees do that.

6. Have employees write the ads that are placed in the newspaper or professional journal.

7. Have employees spend a few hours conducting a realistic job preview. (This is a true-to-life explanation or demonstration of what the job is really about.)

8. Have employees do reference checks. With a little bit of training, it's an educational exercise.

9. Choose one employee as the "Point Person." This is the person who coordinates all activities related to the interviewing process.

10. Have employees contact all of the people who were not offered the job (but were interviewed). Have them establish a personal relationship by phoning. If someone made it as far as the interview process, you want to keep the door open for future opportunities.

FAST STRATEGY #21

Hold Yourself to the Highest Standards

ALTHOUGH THIS SEEMS OBVIOUS, IN THIS day and age of "standards of convenience," it bears repeating. Employees buy into the person first, then the vision. You can't expect employees to have the highest standards if you do not. Employees first care about what you do, not what you say. Although you may be able to cite some examples where this is not the case, for the most part, this holds true.

Employees look at us with a critical eye, which gives us the opportunity to lead by example. Some years ago, I was a human resources (HR) manager, and one of my responsibilities was to develop and conduct soft-skill training programs. One such program was on effective communications. Effective communications is of utmost importance in building a great workplace. The program was attended by all management staff and generally received high marks and much praise.

A few weeks after the program, one of the participants came roaring into my office and demanded to speak with me immediately. My body language showed obvious annoyance, and I said with a combination sweet/sarcastic voice that surely I was doing nothing all day but waiting for him to let me know what my priorities should be. We both looked at each other and then had a good laugh. I figured the air was cleared. However, a week after that, I received some disturbing feedback: "You may be able to teach communications, but you sure can't do what you teach."

That was upsetting, to say the least. And the most upsetting thing was that if I had 99 interactions with this person, they would all be good. It was the one instance that caught me off-guard and where I responded in a less than professional manner that came back to hurt my credibility. One out of 100. The 99 successful interactions only held my credibility within the status quo. The one unsuccessful interaction became the communication that was remembered.

Here are "Four Things to Remember When Holding Yourself to the Highest Standards":

1. Know what your standard is and know what behaviors you can visibly demonstrate so employees will know beyond a shadow of a doubt the standard you adhere to.

2. Base all your interactions in the interest of upholding your standard(s).

3. Understand what is important to your people. They need to be able to easily identify with the standards you're communicating, not only through what you say but also through what you do.

4. Do damage control if you falter (and you will from time to time). Fess up! Recognition that you've fallen from the standard is powerful—everyone else knows it . . . they need to know that you know it, too.

FAST Strategy #22

Communicate for Understanding

E ACH ONE OF US HAS PREFERRED WAYS OF communicating; that is, expressing our thoughts and taking in and processing information. The five senses are the representational systems in neuro-linguistic programming (NLP): visual, auditory, kinesthetic, gustatory, and olfactory. These senses represent what we see, hear, touch or feel, taste, and smell. Interestingly, these systems come into play during our everyday communications. The most common senses are auditory (how we hear things), visual (how we see things), and kinesthetic (how we feel and touch things). For example, if you asked your employees for an opinion on a new attendance policy, they might respond in the following manner:

Visual person—"I can *see* both sides of implementing it."

Auditory person—"I've *heard* that there might be problems with people accepting it."

Kinesthetic person—"I don't *feel* that it will help improve attendance."

Understanding how to present information can greatly enhance communications. Since it is often difficult to determine what someone's preferred method of taking in and processing information might be, it's important to offer information that touches on all modalities. For example:

✦ To capitalize on visual senses: Offer information in writing by using notes, memos, letters, written agendas, flip charts, overheads, Power-Point presentations, or workbooks.

✦ To capitalize on auditory senses: Offer information verbally through two-way discussion—either face to face, by telephone, or by using Web technology—or through tapes, CDs, or lectures.

✦ To capitalize on kinesthetic senses: Offer information that involves the person in the design, use simulations, role-play, case studies, what-if scenarios, or games.

Once you figure out how to best present the information, always check for understanding by using reflecting skills. These include repetition and paraphrasing. Repetition merely gives the person back what was said to you in their words. Paraphrasing allows you to restate what the person has said, putting it in your words. This lets the other person know that you understand the core message, which is critical when crystal-clear communication is needed.

FAST STRATEGY #23

Have a Vision, Take Action

> *Leadership is the capacity to translate*
> *vision into reality.*
> —Warren Bennis

IN JOEL BARKER'S 1991 VIDEO, "THE POWER of Vision," he makes the following statement: "Vision without action is merely a dream. Action without vision just passes the time. Vision with action can change the world." How true.

Your vision manifests itself in a philosophical statement that describes the possible future you see for your department or business unit. It describes the department and its impact on the future and is guided by possibilities and dreams, not constraints. Vision statements are inspirational and give all those affiliated (both internally and externally) with the department something to grab and hold on to. Everything that the department does flows from the vision. And of course, the department's vision statement directly flows from the organization's (if there is one).

This is not to be confused with mission. Mission statements are also philosophical and include the need (values-based) that the department fulfills in the organization and what the department does to meet that need. Mission statements are *brief* and can be easily remembered and internalized by department members. If your organization has a mission statement, yours should flow from that.

What is the vision for your department or business unit? Here are some easy steps to follow to start generating your vision statement:

1. Start by involving everyone in your department. A short brainstorming session is a good starting point and should be done in round-robin fashion so that everyone participates. Generate as many ideas as possible on what main themes should be included in the vision. This is not the time to wordsmith . . . there will be plenty of time for that later!

2. After you've exhausted all ideas, review the list to clarify any ideas that may not be clearly understood by everyone in the group. Then combine similar ideas and eliminate items on the list that are no longer applicable.

3. Use either weighted voting or nominal group technique to determine consensus on the top three or four ideas.

4. Take those top ideas and break into small groups (if the group is large). Come up with a sentence that captures each idea.

5. Put all of the sentences together and start wordsmithing.

6. Voila! You have a vision statement!

After the vision statement is accepted by all members of the department, it should act as your compass, giving guidance and direction to all that you do. The vision statement should be reviewed at least once a year to determine if it still makes sense.

FAST STRATEGY #24

Go to Bat

WITHOUT A DOUBT, BUILDING TRUST AND loyalty in your workforce is a never-ending and difficult job. However, what helps clear the path for an environment of trust is the knowledge that you, as manager, will speak up for your people when they're not able to speak for themselves. This is relatively easy to do when praise is involved. It becomes far more difficult when someone is looking to lay blame for a project or a decision that has run amok.

There are many instances when you'll have the opportunity to go to bat for your team, department, or any one of the employees who works for you. Some instances are:

+ To be innovative or do something in a markedly different way

+ To justify why someone has been assigned to a specific task

+ To justify a position in your department

✦ To give praise to something being done that the rest of the organization has not noticed

✦ To ask for additional resources to enable people to do a better job

✦ To answer for a poorly made decision

✦ To explain why a project is off-track

You get the idea . . . and you probably have dozens more! Use any and all of these situations to get behind your team or employees to fully show your support when they are not able. Make a point to have a mental checklist ready so that when the opportunity presents itself you can readily speak on behalf of those who report to you. And, make sure they know about it. Let your people know that the subject came up (it's not necessary to let them know every negative comment that others might have spoken), and what you had to say about it. Use it as an opportunity to reinforce that you think they're doing well and to correct what they're not doing well. Most of all, let them know that you are behind them 100 percent and that you're ready, willing, and able to let others know the extent of your support.

FAST Strategy #25

Eliminate All Types of Harassment

As WE ENDED THE 1990s, COMPANIES FOUND more and more emphasis being placed on eliminating workplace harassment. In fact, some states mandate antiharassment training. Whether the harassment is sexual, racial, gender-based, or specific to any other type of protected characteristic, one thing is sure—the penalties for not addressing potential and actual situations is substantial. While three of the four Supreme Court decisions of the term that ended in June 1998 gave some guidance (*Faragher v. Boca Raton, Burlington Industries, Inc. v. Ellerth, Oncale v. Sundowner Offshore Services, Inc.*), organizations have still had to wade into many gray areas.

Harassment comes in many forms, from innocent bantering, to pictures, jokes, and actual physical contact, to exchanging favors for job-related benefits. As a supervisor, it's important that you set an environment where all types of harassment are strictly taboo, even those that are unintentional.

Guidelines to help you promote a harassment-free environment are:

✦ Lead by example. Be mindful of what you say and do.

✦ Take appropriate measures to stop harassing behavior.

✦ Provide employees with guidelines of what is acceptable and unacceptable behavior, as per your company policy.

✦ Comply with your organization's stated policy.

✦ Provide answers to employee questions, or find out if you don't know.

✦ Keep written records of any incidences (document, document, document).

✦ Keep human resources or the person or department that oversees this area informed. Forward all documentation to them.

When addressing harassment situations, it's not unusual to be viewed as the bad guy, particularly if you're asking people to refrain from certain language or types of jokes. However, it's far better to be a temporary bad guy than to be embroiled in a major problem six months down the road. If you clearly spell out your intentions, that is, provide employees with the best possible working environment, you may even see your staff take up the antiharassment cause.

FAST STRATEGY #26

Help Raise Your Employees' EQ . . . and Yours Too!

Fᴏʀ Mᴇɴsᴀ-ʟɪᴋᴇ sᴄʜᴏʟᴀʀs, ᴛʜᴇ ɴᴇᴡs ɪs not good. EQ is quickly replacing IQ as the hot commodity skill. You can help your employers and employees by raising EQ. What is EQ? It's your emotional intelligence quotient, which results in emotional competency.

Emotional intelligence is a mixture of social skills, social awareness, self-awareness, and self-management combined with your ability to use these qualities in a positive way when interacting with others. In short, it's the ability to control and express your emotions, and it can encompass a wide breadth of personality-type traits.

Reams of research are available on this subject. Daniel Goleman, Ph.D., defines *emotional competency* as "a learned capability based on emotional intelligence that results in outstanding performance at work." Goleman is the author of several books, most notably his 1995 book titled *Emotional Intelligence*. (Admittedly, there are people who are in disagreement with Goleman.)

This concept has significant implications for management and employees alike. If you're management, this can fundamentally change how you hire and develop people. Suddenly, EQ becomes more important than task knowledge. This may change the way interviews are done, job descriptions are written, performance is evaluated, and promotions and pay increases are given. The training focus shifts from hard skills to soft skills.

For your employees, EQ may change how they view their role in the organization and what they need to accomplish in order to maintain or change career paths. Everyday interactions and communications take on added value. Skills such as problem solving, conflict management, the ability to handle change, and working well in small project teams have greater value in the career equation.

The bottom line is that there is data to support that people with higher EQs are more successful in the workplace. Cary Cherniss, Ph.D., from the Rutgers Graduate School of Applied and Professional Psychology, published a paper that found the following examples of EQ successes (there were 15 more examples):

1. A consulting firm assessed experienced partners on a variety of emotional intelligence competencies. Partners scoring above the median on 9 or more of the 20 competencies delivered

$1.2 million more profit from their accounts than did other partners—a 139 percent incremental gain (Boyatzis, R. E., from a presentation to the Linkage Conference on Emotional Intelligence, Chicago, IL, September 27, 1999).

2. At a national furniture retailer, salespeople hired based on emotional competence had half the dropout rate during their first year (Hay/McBer Research and Innovation Group, 1997).

3. Research by the Center for Creative Leadership has found that the primary causes of derailment in executives involve deficits in emotional competence. The three primary ones are difficulty in handling change, not being able to work well in a team, and poor interpersonal relations.

So, if you're looking to take yourself, your employees, and the organization to the next level . . . work smarter, not harder, and increase those EQ points!

FAST STRATEGY #27

Grin, Win, and Have Some Fun

MOST OF US ARE FAMILIAR WITH HOOTERS, an establishment known for the "Hooters Girls." At a Panama City Beach Hooters, the manager held a contest in April 2001 to see who could sell the most beer. The top-selling waitresses from each area Hooters were entered into a drawing for a new Toyota. (Most of us would be very pleased about that kind of reward and recognition!)

Waitress Jodee Berry was announced the winner. She was taken blindfolded into the parking lot, eagerly anticipating her new car. The blindfold was removed, and before her was a new . . . Toy Yoda. For her efforts, she was the proud owner of a Star Wars Yoda doll. Needless to say, Berry was not amused, although she reported that her manager was inside the restaurant laughing. In fact, she quit her job a week later and sued, alleging fraudulent misrepresentation and breach of contract. What was she looking for? The cost of a new Toyota.

We hear from experts (and nonexperts, too!) that we should make our organizations more fun. In fact, programs like FiSH! (from the book *FiSH! A Remarkable Way to Boost Morale and Improve Results*, by Steven Lundin, Ph.D, Harry Paul, and John Christensen) are taking the workplace by storm. Two of the major points in the FiSH! program are to Choose Your Attitude and Play. In the context of FiSH!, this is great, especially if you're looking to capture the synergy of your workforce and channel it toward better teamwork, customer service, and profitability.

The problem starts when the "fun" isn't fun for everyone. It really comes back to treating employees fairly and ethically, and building a workplace culture steeped in trust and integrity. It starts with the manager, or highest-ranking senior leader, and trickles down throughout the entire organization.

Grinning and winning (having some fun while achieving great results) is a wonderful plus in any workplace. To make sure that it doesn't get too out of hand, be aware of the following guidelines.

Do's

+ Gauge what is acceptable by asking employees. Involve them in the process.

+ Good, clean fun is almost always in style. If you don't believe me, just look at comedians like Sinbad and Bill Cosby.

+ Self-deprecating humor is usually okay, as long as it's not taken to the extreme.

✦ Watch the body language reaction of others. Often people won't say that a comment, joke, or behavior is bothersome, but their body language may indicate otherwise. Watch for changes in body posture, eye contact, facial expression, and participation in the conversation. These could signal unwelcome behavior.

✦ People should feel good about having fun. Watch for smiles.

✦ Be a leader in having fun. Special theme days, department lunches, and Secret Santas need to have your participation.

Don'ts

✦ Offensive, off-color, or otherwise questionable conduct is never acceptable.

✦ Don't encourage anything that you wouldn't want on the front page of the newspaper.

✦ Don't rush or require people to participate. Participation from everyone may come slowly. They'll eventually become involved when it appears to be more fun to be involved than not to be involved.

✦ Avoid jokes or humor directed at others.

Remember, employees will take their cues from you!

FAST STRATEGY #28

Develop Leaders,
Not Followers

I

IN THE WORKPLACE, WE TALK ABOUT DEVEL-
oping leadership skills, but it seems reserved mostly
for managers. Being a manager doesn't automatically
bestow upon you leadership status, although it's a
good bet that you stand a better chance of being put
in the leadership role if you are in the management
ranks. An opportunity we miss is to develop leadership skills in the employees who report to us.

When we develop selected managers, we are literally taking baby steps in the leadership cycle. However, when we teach leaders how to develop leaders,
we take the proverbial quantum leap.

In *The 21 Irrefutable Laws of Leadership*, author John
Maxwell talks about The Law of Explosive Growth
(Law 20). Maxwell says, "You will go to the highest
level only if you begin developing leaders instead of
followers." He then talks about leader's math. With
leader's math, the equation becomes simple. For

example, for every follower you add, you reap a relative increase in the growth of your organization. Ten good followers give you the power of 10 good people. For every leader you add, you not only have the power that leader brings to the table but also the power of the followers and leaders he or she influences. The addition of 10 good leaders results in exponential growth, all for the same effort as developing followers!

What does this mean to your organization? Focus on not only teaching leadership skills, but also on teaching your leaders how to teach leadership skills to their employees. This is a good place to start, but as Randall White, Philip Hodgeson, and Stuart Crainer wrote in *The Future of Leadership*, "The rapid rise, and fall, of companies has shown that one good idea will get you going, but a succession of good ideas is needed to keep you in business." So it goes with keeping leaders in your business. Here are a few things to think about:

- ✦ Do you have the resources to devote to leadership development? Can you afford not to devote the resources to gain exponential growth and a competitive advantage?

- ✦ Is your organization ready to shift its focus and change the culture into one that expects leadership from all?

- ✦ What role will the CEO and all senior leadership have instilling this throughout the organization?

♦ What measurable outcomes will you put into place? How will you know that your foray into leaders leading leaders has been successful?

To take that quantum leap in your own career, develop leadership skills in others.

FAST Strategy #29

Use Recognition That Works

Say good-bye to "Employee of the Month." Bid a fond adieu to five-year pins. Name in the newsletter? Auf wiedersehen and good night! Do you think that's all employees need to feel recognized? If so, it's time to think again!

It is critical for organizations to retain top talent, now more than ever. One way is through individual recognition. Recognizing employees en masse has become routine, watered-down, and in the words of one manager, "Ho-hum."

At a management seminar I conducted, we were discussing best practices for rewarding and recognizing employees. The inevitable question was posed. *"Just what is the best way to recognize employees?"* Gathering all the wisdom of the past 20 years, I answered, *"It all depends."* Of course the person who asked the question wanted to know what "it" was dependent upon. My answer: *"Dependent on the individual employee."*

I then asked each person to list his or her employees and how each employee liked to be recognized. Not one person could definitively answer that question. How do you find out? The answer is deceptively simple.

Ask. Involve. Check. Ask again. And again.

Bob Nelson, author of several best-selling books, including *1001 Ways to Reward Employees*, made the following comment regarding recognition. "Raise the awareness of your managers about the importance of them appreciating their employees on a daily basis when they do good work—one-on-one or via voice mail, in writing or e-mail, in meetings . . . The rewards that are most beneficial to any employee are the ones they want! Find out what those might be by asking them in one or more ways. It very well may not be "stuff" at all, but perhaps autonomy, flexibility, trust, support, visibility, opportunity, and so forth."

Start by asking your employees what's meaningful to them—how they'd like to be recognized. Involve them in the process that affects them. After you've recognized them in their preferred manner, check back to see if it was truly meaningful. Did they like it? At periodic intervals, ask again . . . and again. Great recognition programs quickly become meaningless recognition programs when we stop asking employees what they want.

Here's what one employee of a local company says, "My manager thanks me 10 times a day, for doing things that are really just a part of my job. That means a lot to me and motivates me to work even more conscientiously. He is genuinely grateful for the work I do."

It's not necessarily about money, formal programs, or getting your name in the company newsletter. It's all about what matters to each individual employee.

FAST STRATEGY #30

Mentor

O NE OF THE MOST SUCCESSFUL WAYS TO develop your employees is to step up the mentoring program. Mentoring programs can be either formal or informal and can involve one or more mentors, including yourself. The word *mentor* has its origins in Homer's *Odyssey*. Mentor was Odysseus' wise and trusted counselor, in whose form Athena became the teacher of Odysseus' son, Telemachus. According to *The American Heritage® Dictionary of the English Language, Fourth Edition*, the word *mentor* means "a wise and trusted counselor or teacher" or "to serve as a trusted counselor or teacher, especially in occupational settings."

In a mentoring relationship there is a pairing of the mentor(s) and the mentee or protégé. While it is possible to have an informal mentoring relationship, for best results start out with a formal relationship. Mentors should have the following qualities:

✦ Good listening skills

✦ Good feedback skills

+ Good assessment skills

+ Proficiency in the competency area where he or she will be mentoring

+ Ability to tap into a variety of resources to help the mentee

+ High level of commitment to the mentoring relationship

Mentees or protégés should have the following qualities:

+ Results oriented—the desire to set goals and achieve them in a timely way

+ Self-direction—the ability to take responsibility for one's own development

+ Commitment to use the feedback given by the mentor

+ High level of commitment to the mentoring relationship

Before starting any mentoring relationship, come to an agreement regarding the goals and expectations of the relationship. Put it in writing and refer to it often. Decide on the following:

+ What skills or competencies does the mentee want to attain?

+ How can the mentor assist?

+ How will confidential issues be handled?

✦ How often will you meet?

✦ How long will the relationship last?

✦ How will you assess progress and determine success?

Mentoring relationships can help develop your employees in a way that training programs cannot. The relationship can deal with skill development in a timely way and give immediate feedback, direction, and guidance. Not everyone is cut out to be a mentor, but if you are, this just might help build your staff and enhance the workplace environment.

FAST Strategy #31

Understand Coaching Responsibilities

Are you a boss or a coach? Bosses dictate, order, make sure the work gets done, and provide directions on what to do. Coaches mentor, teach, help others to become self-directed, and offer direction and context so people understand what to do. It makes sense that if you want to build and sustain long-lasting high performance in your workforce, then the way to do it is by coaching rather than by bossing. Some of the responsibilities of a coach are given below.

To Build the Competency Levels of Staff

Coaches clearly state what the expected competency level of staff should be and hold each person accountable for meeting or exceeding that standard. A good coach can help an employee pinpoint where he or she is in professional development, define what needs to be done to reach higher levels, and provide two-way feedback. Coaches raise the performance standard as needed and recognize those who exceed the standard. Coaches go to bat for their people.

To Open Up Possibilities So People Can Think Creatively

Coaches look to the edges of the organization and are constantly on the lookout for new ways of doing things. A coach challenges each person to do the same and gives "gentle pushes" to achieve goals. Brainstorming, "what if" statements, and other creative-thinking techniques are routinely introduced and used. Coaches do not make statements like "We've always done it this way" or "It won't work."

To Assist with Breakdowns When Needed

Coaches help their people to map the process, locate the breakdown, and then clear the path. They help in generating solutions. A coach offers guidance in anticipating the next breakdown and developing ways to avoid it. The coach keeps the focus on the issue, not on any individual's personal shortcomings.

FAST STRATEGY #32

Understand How to Coach for CHANGE

COACHES ATTEMPT TO EFFECT SOME TYPE OF behavioral change in an individual or a team. What are the elements needed to set the stage for change? CHANGE is an acronym that stands for the important elements needed for a successful coaching intervention:

+ **C**ontract

+ **H**andle Difficulties

+ **A**ssess and Approach

+ **N**egate the Old

+ **G**ive Reinforcement

+ **E**valuate and Make Changes

Let's look at these in more detail.

Contract

The first step involves contracting with the individual to build a foundation for the change to occur. This step is key in a successful coaching intervention. A coaching contract is similar to any type of contract: It sets the tone with a clear, workable agreement. When constructing the coaching contract consider the following:

✦ Do all parties share the same understanding of all the terms and conditions of the contract?

✦ Is the intended outcome or goal stated?

✦ How will attaining or accomplishing this goal be measured?

✦ What are the action steps?

✦ What is the schedule for each step?

✦ Who is accountable for each step along the way?

✦ Who are the players?

✦ What is the feedback mechanism? How does it work?

✦ What follow-up will occur?

Handle Difficulties

It is not unusual for a coach to encounter difficulties, both from the person or people who are being coached and from outside participants. To ensure that the intervention does not become derailed along the way, consider the following:

✦ What difficulties do you anticipate before even starting the intervention? What strategies can you put into place to be proactive in handling these situations?

✦ Do you have a toolbag? If so, do you have all of your tools handy? If not, when will you start building one?

✦ How will you know what resistance looks like? Defensiveness? Anxiety? How will you handle these?

✦ How will you behave if criticized? How will you distinguish if it is a valid criticism of the intervention or an attack on you?

✦ What follow-up mechanism will you put into place? How will you monitor progress?

Assess and Approach

Once you have agreed on the contract and considered how to handle difficulties, it's time to design a coaching approach. It's important to know the person or people you are working with, and then develop appropriate coaching strategies. One size definitely does not fit all!

✦ What is the primary situation that has to be rectified? Is this really the problem? Are there other issues that must be addressed to get to the real problem?

✦ What tools will you use to assess the situation? (interviews, pencil and paper instruments, data collection methods)

✦ What is your style? What is the style of the person or team with whom you are working? What approach is most appropriate given the two styles?

✦ Has anything like this been done in the past? Successes? Failures?

✦ What is your time frame?

✦ Will other people be a part of this?

Negate the Old

Negate means "to neutralize, cancel, or counteract." And that's exactly what coaches are trying to do . . . cancel the old, unacceptable behaviors and replace them with new, acceptable behaviors. But, old habits die hard . . . and as human beings we are very much invested in our old ways, even if those old ways yield negative results. In trying to help an employee or team break those old habits, ask yourself these questions:

✦ Does this person realize his or her patterns? Do you?

✦ What will motivate this person to break the old habits and replace them with new habits?

✦ Is this something that can be done solo or will additional assistance be required?

✦ Can you describe this in quantifiable terms?

✦ How can you discuss this so that emotion does not take over?

✦ What type of follow-up mechanism will be used?

Give Reinforcement

Reinforcement is key in making the new habits stick and getting the type of behavior change you seek. There are many different types of reinforcers. A good coach needs to find the ones that work best. As a note, positive reinforcers are generally more effective in sustaining long-term behavior changes.

Behavior modification, based on the work of B. F. Skinner, is a program that focuses on managing human activity by controlling the consequences of performing that activity.

✦ Positive reinforcement is a reward that consists of a desirable consequence of behavior.

✦ Negative reinforcement is a reward that consists of the elimination of an undesirable consequence.

✦ Punishment is the presentation of an undesirable behavioral consequence or the removal of a desirable one that decreases the likelihood that the behavior will continue.

Evaluate and Make Changes

As with any course of action, it is important in a coaching intervention to evaluate what is occurring and to make changes to ensure success (as much as possible). The goal, of course, is to have some quantifiable measurement so that you, as a coach, can measure if any change has occurred and to what extent.

✦ Is your evaluation or measurement mechanism working?

✦ Has the original outcome or goal been achieved?

✦ If so, how will you maintain the gain?

✦ If not, what are your options? What is the next step?

✦ Has the schedule been followed? Have there been changes?

✦ Have there been process measurements along the way? What have those measurements shown?

✦ Is the employee motivated and committed to improving performance?

FAST Strategy #33

Establish Goals and Have Frequent Goal Meetings

In absence of clearly defined goals, we become strangely loyal to performing daily acts of trivia.
—Anonymous

SETTING GOALS IS AN EASY PROCESS. ACHIEVing them, however, is not always so easy. One of the easiest ways is to use the tried and true SMART goal formula. Help employees set and reach goals by using the SMART acronym:

Specific—What needs to be done? What result is desired? Are the goals clearly delineated?

Measurable—How will you measure success? How will you know the goal has been met?

Attainable or Action-Oriented—Can the goals be accomplished with reasonable resources? Is it within reach with just a bit of stretching?

Relevant or Realistic—Is the goal part of what's important in the organization? Can the employee expect to contribute to the bigger picture by successfully completing the goal?

Timely—When will the goal be completed? Is there a solid commitment to a deadline?

By assisting employees to establish and accomplish important goals, you help to enhance their commitment, motivation, and self-directedness toward the job. It's important to remember, though, that setting goals is not enough. Frequent meetings are important to:

✦ Review progress on goals

✦ Revise goals as organizational priorities dictate

✦ Work through roadblocks

✦ Brainstorm different approaches

✦ Celebrate upon goal completion

✦ Establish new goals

Employees often have conflicting priorities and can spend much of their time on nonessential and nonproductive work. It is your job, as supervisor, to help redirect employees to the "vital few" tasks, rather than having them spend their time on the "trivial many." This is also called the 80/20 concept or the Pareto Principle (J. M. Juran, *Managerial Breakthrough*). Some examples of the 80/20 concept are 80 percent of absenteeism is caused by 20 percent of the employees, or 20 percent of the people do 80 percent of the talking in any given group. When it comes to working on goals, very often 80 percent of our employees' effort gets spent on only 20 percent of the critical work, and important goals fall by the wayside. It's very easy to get caught up in day-to-day crises, and very soon progress on goals comes to a halt.

That's why it's important to meet on a regular basis with employees and keep them focused on the vital few goals—those goals that will have greatest organizational impact when completed. Very soon, when the sense of accomplishment takes hold, your employees will start to pick up the ball and take responsibility for goal setting and completion.

FAST STRATEGY #34

Know What Your Competition Is Doing

To PARAPHRASE (AND SLIGHTLY CHANGE) A famous quote: "Keep your employees close, but keep your competition closer!" While it's important for you to understand employees and their productivity, it's just as important to have a thorough understanding of those who might influence your employees' decision to leave the company.

Before you can even think about what the competition is doing, know who the competition is. For example, a large nonprofit company felt that its competition for residential staff was other similar nonprofits. Indeed, many former employees seemed to go to these other nonprofits on a regular basis; however, when former residential employees were surveyed, it was found that the greatest majority of this group went to completely different industries, such as retail and fast-food. The other nonprofits were not the competition; the true competitors for the employee base were Wal-Mart, Burger King, and McDonald's.

Having this information allows you to gather better information on what attracts and retains employees in the workplace. Try to be knowledgeable in at least the following areas:

✦ What are the demographics of your competitors' workforces?

✦ What is the average tenure of employment?

✦ What attracts employees to your competition?

✦ How does your company's pay and benefits compare with the competition's?

✦ What special perks does the competition offer that you don't?

✦ What differentiates your competitor's workplace environment from yours?

✦ What are the primary and secondary reasons that people leave your company, and how is that satisfied with the new employer?

The answers to these questions will get you started in providing employees with the type of environment that is conducive to long-term employment. Granted, some of these areas require a long-term commitment to change; however, it all starts with asking the right questions and then using the answers to build a strong foundation.

FAST Strategy #35

Conduct Effective Department and Team Meetings

W HY DO WE HAVE MEETINGS AT ALL? MEET-
ings can be useful, and in fact productive, if done correctly. Meetings are primarily held because an issue
requires the interaction of different people with different perspectives to be solved. Also, group buy-in
may be essential.

Do any of the following meeting problems sound
familiar?

+ Getting off the subject

+ No goals or agenda

+ Too lengthy

+ Poor or inadequate preparation

+ Inconclusive

✦ Disorganized

✦ Ineffective leadership or lack of control

✦ Irrelevance of information discussed

✦ Time wasted during meetings

✦ Starting late

✦ Not effective for decision making

✦ Interruptions

✦ Dominating individuals

✦ Rambling or digressive discussion

✦ No written results or follow-up action

✦ No pre-meeting orientation/canceled or post-poned meetings

—Source: *Rochester Institute of Technology, 1992*

There *is* a cure!

Productive meetings that people actually don't mind attending require a bit of work. Before the meeting, do some careful planning. Determine who needs to be at the meeting, where and when it will be held, and the general purpose of the meeting. Send out agendas ahead of time so participants can be prepared. And, since you're the chairperson, it's important for you to be there a little early to make sure everything is in order.

Start meetings on time, or as close to the scheduled time as possible. Know how long the meeting will last and end it on time. Quickly review the agenda and make any necessary corrections. If needed, assign roles, such as secretary or recorder, timekeeper, or facilitator. Follow the agenda, stay on track, and ensure that all people at the meeting are participating.

Before the meeting ends, establish action items, review achievements, and schedule the next meeting date. If it makes sense, you can even set the agenda or parts of it. Also, you may want to put into place an evaluation mechanism to assess the effectiveness of the meeting.

Have the minutes prepared and distributed to all participants shortly after the meeting. And, prior to the next meeting, gently remind people about action items that were assigned to them.

When your meetings start and end on time and people attending feel that they've contributed and accomplished something, the negative connotation of "yet another meeting" will start to fade.

FAST Strategy #36

Understand Different Strategies for Dealing with Conflict

Forming, Storming, Norming, and Performing. These are the stages of team development as defined by Bruce Tuckman in the 1965 *Psychological Bulletin* article "Developmental Sequence in Small Groups," and refined by Mary Ann Jensen with the addition of the Adjourning stage in 1977.

Forming is the first stage of the team development process. Team members explore issues, expectations, roles and rules, authority, and what skills fellow team members may possess. The Forming stage might be characterized as the "honeymoon" stage, with feelings of excitement, anxiety, fear, and anticipation . . . all at the same time!

Storming is the second stage and is characterized by conflict about roles and rules, and disagreement regarding team direction. There may be frustration with other team members and the work itself. Defensiveness and confrontation are commonplace. Attendance at team meetings or other team venues may be a problem, and team members may start to question their own commitment to the team as well as the commitment of other team members. To get beyond this stage, it is critical for managers to encourage honest, open, and respectful discussion about disagreements.

The third stage of team development is *Norming*. Here, we find agreement about roles and rules, and what constitutes acceptable behaviors. Team members are likely to feel an openness in discussing new ideas and begin to focus on a common goal. There is a feeling of team spirit. Team members initiate and participate in open discussions regarding team dynamics.

Teams in the fourth stage of team development, or the *Performing* stage, tend to focus on solving organizational or team-mandated issues. This is a stage of high performance. There is easy adaptation to change and a closeness among team members. Each person derives a feeling of satisfaction from participating in the team. There is recognition, which is important to reinforcing productive team behavior and to enhancing the likelihood that it will continue in the future. Team members feel a sense of belonging and derive a sense of status from their affiliation with the team. Not all teams reach the Performing stage.

Lastly is the fifth stage of team development, or the *Adjourning* stage. At this point, the team is finishing its job and preparing to disband. This stage normally occurs in teams established for some special purpose for a limited time. Team members may feel disappointment or a sense of loss, especially if the team was in the Performing stage, so this is a good time to take measures to recognize each person's contributions. Evaluate and document the team's work, achievements, and lessons learned. Develop a way to maintain the gains and share results with the organization.

The Forming, Norming, and Performing stages usually run fairly smoothly. It's the Storming stage that takes up much of our time as managers and that has undermined the efforts of many teams. It's important to understand that every team goes through a Storming stage—even the ones that don't admit it. The most successful teams understand that Storming is a normal part of team development, and they effectively deal with the conflict during this stage.

There can be good reason for team conflict, so it's important to move in a positive and proactive way to reduce conflict and get the group back on track. Try some of the following strategies:

✦ Try to deal with the underlying reasons for conflict; use active listening skills.

✦ Be aware of what team members are doing outside of work. If a team member goes to an extreme, there may be problems outside of work that are causing the conflict.

✦ Use subgroups or joint job assignments to help reduce conflict.

✦ Some conflicts between dominant people may need to be dealt with outside the group.

✦ Focus on the positive side of each person's differences. Each person brings a different strength to the table.

✦ If possible, redesign the job to maximize the group's effectiveness.

✦ If you are dealing with multiple conflicts, start with the one that seems easiest to resolve. Go for the quick victory to set a tone of success in conflict resolution.

✦ Do not overlook the possibility that you may be causing or exacerbating the conflict.

✦ If you want your team to be high-performance, as the Team Leader or Supervisor you also need to be in a high-performance mode.

✦ People often try to achieve solidarity by attacking a scapegoat, either within or outside the group. This is damaging, and the group should be redirected.

✦ If necessary, bring in a third person to act as a mediator.

Not all conflict is bad—a moderate amount of conflict is healthy and essential to a well-functioning team. Do not take any of these hints too far or so literally that they do more harm than good. The techniques and information provided here are guidelines. You need to use judgment when implementing them with your group.

FAST STRATEGY #37

Help Employees Develop a "Big Picture" Focus

An underlying principle of Tae Kwon Do states that by understanding the larger perspective, or the big picture, all the details will fall into place. Those skilled in this martial art can handle several attackers at one time. Why? Because the martial artist is reacting to the big picture (all attackers!), rather than worrying about how to throw a punch.

One of the most valuable skills that any individual can bring to an employer is the ability to maintain perspective on the big picture. This is something that every manager can help employees develop. I once had a boss and mentor say to me, "When you're up to your ears in alligators, sometimes it's hard to remember that your mission is to drain the swamp." At that time, I was immersed in a project and fretting over some of the details. He felt that I was spending way too much time on those details and not enough time focusing on my true mission. It's those people who can hold on to the mission, who don't get "mired in the minutiae," who will be perceived as most valuable to the organization.

Here are six important questions to consider when working with employees:

1. Are you helping your organization achieve strategic, operational, and financial advantage through what you do? If you can't answer yes to all three, then think about how your job is structured and what can be done to restructure it.

2. Do you have hard performance measures? Are they based on hard data, and are those measures tied to the organization's strategy? Can you easily show the value that you bring to the organization?

3. Do you take a continuous improvement approach to your job, or do you rest on laurels from past successes? Do you know when good enough is good enough?

4. Do you keep customers (whether internal or external) at the forefront of your thinking? Do they drive what you do?

5. Do you know how to use technology for competitive advantage? Do you know how to successfully meld "high tech" and "high touch"?

6. Are you an expert in your part of the organization? Do you share that expertise and are you a resource for others?

The answers to these questions will give you an indication of where your employees' focus is directed. Answering no to any question means that the focus may not be on the bigger picture. When the focus is on the smaller aspects of the organization, the value that each employee brings to the organization decreases. It doesn't matter if that person is a cashier, vice president, or a health-care professional. Knowing where each employee fits into the big picture, and how to maximize the contribution within that context, can mean the difference between a big return or a little to no return. Help employees keep their collective eye on the big picture and watch the details fall into place.

FAST STRATEGY #38

Get Rid of the Fickle Finger of Blame

T HE FICKLE FINGER OF BLAME IS AN INSIDIOUS by-product of a work environment steeped in disrespect, low morale, and resistance to trying new and different approaches. The fickle finger of blame inevitably lands on an individual when something has gone wrong and someone has to take the fall or answer to a higher authority (usually your boss). And, you never know when it might land on you.

Accountability and responsibility are admirable attributes to cultivate in all your employees; pointing the fickle finger of blame does not encourage these attributes. In fact, it helps promote the CYA (Cover Your Butt) mentality. Let me give you an example of how this works.

A few years ago, two human resources (HR) professionals were put in charge of a major salary administration overhaul. Part of this overhaul involved rewriting all existing job descriptions. This was no easy task, as there were over 100 job titles. The two HR people tried to involve as many employees and supervisors as possible in the rewrites, and also took into account what executive management wanted. Finally the job description rewrites were completed and distributed. What followed was completely unexpected.

There was an outcry that the job descriptions did not accurately reflect the jobs. So the CEO sat down with the two HR professionals and said it was important for the three of them to apologize to the employees at the next meeting and to assure them that the job descriptions would go back to the drawing board. The CEO felt it was important for them to take responsibility for what had gone wrong.

The two HR people got up at the next meeting and made the public apology. The CEO was conspicuously absent, having successfully pointed the fickle finger of blame in their direction. Needless to say, these two individuals were much more guarded about how they went about their work in the future and approached their work with a CYA mentality.

Had the CEO approached the problem in a more positive, less accusatory, and less demoralizing way, the two HR people probably would be more inclined to try new things and take some calculated risks. However, they now approach tasks more cautiously: "How can I cover myself in case we have a problem?"

Here's a positive way to deal with getting rid of the fickle finger of blame. A few years ago, Remedy Corporation wanted to encourage an environment of risk-taking. Although some companies might choose to reward and recognize individuals or teams that were successful in taking risks, Remedy took it one step further. Each employee received one "Take a Chance" card. Managers got more. These were used when an employee took a risk that didn't pan out. No punishment. No negativity. No sweat. Employees are expected to take risks in their jobs, and managers are expected to take even more risks.

Here's an organization that has truly minimized, and perhaps eliminated, the fickle finger of blame. Try these ideas to get you started:

✦ Have an expectation that employees will try new things, and if they don't work out, visibly recognize their efforts in trying something new.

✦ Never criticize or humiliate employees. You're dealing with the work, not the individuals doing the work.

✦ Use the SIMPLE feedback formula (FAST Strategy #17) to debrief when things run amok.

✦ Demonstrate, in some tangible way, that you are getting rid of placing blame. Emphasize that you are all there to work together and act as resources for one another. Some tangible actions might be:

  ✦ "Take a Risk" or "Get-Out-of-Jail" cards.

  ✦ Hold a ceremony that buries the fickle finger of blame.

◆ Establish guidelines or ground rules that prevent the fickle finger of blame from landing on anyone.

◆ Promote positive reinforcement for efforts.

◆ Contract as partners to resolve projects or programs that have gone poorly.

FAST STRATEGY #39

Lead the Change in Thinking

*If in the last few years you haven't discarded
a major opinion or acquired a new one,
check your pulse. You may be dead.*
—Gelett Burgess, 1866–1951

P USH YOURSELF TO THE OUTER LIMITS OF YOUR organization. When change is inevitable (and isn't it always?), it is seldom from the core. It is not from those who are heavily invested in the old way of doing things. Changes come from those who have nothing to lose by trying something new.

Think about your own investment in "the way it's always been" thinking. Companies like Intel and Microsoft; people like Alexander Graham Bell and Dr. W. Edwards Deming; advances in health care, like out-patient surgery; or 24-hour sports or news coverage on stations like ESPN or CNN are a result of changes that occurred on the fringes. No one person in the core group was responsible for leading the way. Certainly Microsoft and Intel have given us a completely new philosophy in fast, efficient technology for the masses. Alexander Graham Bell was not in the mainstream of communications. Dr. W. Edwards Deming had to go to Japan for acceptance of his ideas on total quality. And ESPN and CNN were not born of the mainstream news and sports media of the day.

In a time when work process, technology, and information change at lightning speed, our thought processes are lagging far behind. To set the tone for a change in thinking, try the following exercise:

1. First, identify three or four significant changes that you've witnessed in your organization over the last three to five years. Where did those changes originate? Remember, just because a CEO mandates a new policy or program, it doesn't mean the change originated from that person. Look beyond the confines of the organization to determine the point of origin.

2. Once you've identified the changes and understand where they originated, ask yourself these questions:

   ✦ From what direction are the next changes likely to occur? (Remember, look to the fringes.)

   ✦ What actions will you take?

✦ What impact might this change have on your organization or department?

✦ What will the impact be if the change occurs and you take no action?

3. Decide, with input from your staff, what to anticipate and what type of action is appropriate to take.

FAST STRATEGY #40

Help Your People Adapt to Change

H ELPING YOUR EMPLOYEES ADAPT TO change requires you to be the Change Agent. The Change Agent is the person who leads the change. The changes that you are orchestrating may be narrow (implementing a new time-card system) or broad (altering the culture of an organization). Regardless of the magnitude of the change, Change Agents have common characteristics:

+ Ability to relate to diverse groups of people

+ Ability to determine how a change should be made

+ Problem-solving skills

+ Persuasive influence skills

+ Ability to determine how much change employees can withstand

+ Ability to match internal organizational strengths and weaknesses with external opportunities and threats (FAST Strategy #4)

+ Flexibility and responsiveness to change

What happens to organizations when people don't adapt to change? Depending on the stability of the organization and the time it takes to adapt, there are several possible outcomes.

S T A B I L I T Y	When stability is high and adaptation time is low, the result is a slow, and sometimes tortuous, death.	When stability is high and adaptation time is high, the result is ability to survive downturns . . . and subsequent growth.
	When both stability and adaptation time are low, the result is quick death.	When stability is low and adaptation time is high, the result is a false sense of security followed by a quick death.

ADAPTATION TIME

There are many in-between variations and combinations. This points out the need to not only provide a stable organization, but also to be highly adaptable to change. These guidelines will help you start breaking down the barriers:

+ Keep the information flowing to your employees. No surprises.

◆ Promote understanding through two-way communication and active listening skills.

◆ Answer questions as honestly as possible.

◆ Walk the talk. Be a Change Agent. Set the tone to positively reinforce whenever possible.

◆ Cascade a positive attitude.

◆ Work incrementally. Make small-scale changes first. Use trial runs.

◆ Go for a quick win to build momentum.

FAST STRATEGY #41

Look for Opportunities to Develop Employees' Skills

T HERE'S BARELY A DAY THAT GOES BY WHEN we don't hear about the skills and competencies employees need to develop to take the organization into the future. While intellectually we agree with statements like these, it's more difficult to translate that premise into tangible actions.

One organization I'm familiar with has made this a priority. Employees are regularly assessed in terms of current strengths and developmental needs. These competencies are related to future job opportunities that the employee might aspire to in coming years. Employees find out what competencies they already have that are needed for future job opportunities, and where they must develop additional competencies. Then a plan is put into place to give employees the resources to work on their developmental needs.

If you don't have this type of formalized, company-wide program you can establish one by starting with benchmarking from this best practice. Don't wait for a formal program; look for the opportunity to home-grow your employees' skills.

Use the following steps to formulate your own program:

1. Write down the specific skills and competencies needed to take your department to the next level.

2. Assess, in conjunction with the employee, his or her strengths and developmental needs. Use a pencil-and-paper or online assessment if possible.

3. Compare, in chart form, the skills you need, what the employee has, and what is needed.

4. Review with the employee and develop a feasible plan, using SMART goals (FAST Strategy #33).

5. Review on a regular basis and provide ongoing feedback.

Here's an example of how this can work. In a discussion with an employee, a manager discovered that the employee was bored. This came as a surprise, as the employee was a top producer; there was a high degree of work quality and quantity. The manager started discussing the future of the department. One of the important functions was project monitoring, which involved knowledge in project management, especially budgeting. During the discussion, the manager found out that the employee had a financial analysis background. Together, the manager and employee developed a plan that would allow the employee involvement in project monitoring without being overwhelmed with current job duties.

It was also discovered that the employee was weak in some specific computer skills that were needed, so the manager arranged for additional one-on-one training. Regular follow-up was scheduled. The end result was an employee who continued to be a solid contributor to the old job, was motivated by the challenges of the new duties, and a manager who didn't have to go to outside resources to satisfy departmental needs. The manager, the employee, and the company all benefited from this process.

FAST Strategy #42

Find the Jewel (When the Clouds Are Dark)

THERE'S A TOP-SELLING INSURANCE SALES-person who consistently ranks as a super salesperson in his company. Each time I see him, we greet each other with, "How's it going?" And each time he says something to the effect of, "Absolutely, fantastically great!"

Sometimes I know that things aren't going great. New business could be off, longtime customers may be switching to another agent, or there might be personal problems that are demanding his attention. But that doesn't seem to matter. One of the secrets to my insurance buddy's success is that he's consistently able to find the jewel.

Keeping focus on the positive—finding the jewel—can determine whether your employees have high or low morale. Most employees expect to deal with a variety of workplace issues, such as layoffs, salary cuts, unfair policies and practices, and decisions that seem to have no rhyme or reason. Employees also realize that you may not have any control over various situations. The key is to let your employees know that you understand their points of view and then focus on how to deal with the situation in a positive way.

For example, one manager suggests, "Commiserate and take action." If there is a policy or procedure change that doesn't make sense but must be implemented, this manager tells employees that it doesn't make any sense to her either, but it has to be done, so let's figure out the best way. Some senior leaders may see this as not supporting the company, but this manager of the year argues it's just the opposite. "Employees can see right through bad decisions. Saying that I'm behind it is dishonest, and it doesn't build a relationship with employees."

Try these suggestions:

✦ When there is negativity all around, call the group together for a brainstorming session to identify the positives. Then, set quick, attainable goals to reap the rewards of the positive items you've identified.

✦ Brainstorm the negatives. Look at what the group can and can't control. Develop improvement plans for those that are controllable; develop "live with it" plans for those that aren't controllable. The important thing is to not spend any more time or energy on the uncontrollable issues than is absolutely necessary.

✦ Implement a department suggestion program, with meaningful rewards. Nonfinancial rewards work quite well.

✦ Implement a "penalty" system for negativity, similar to the fines many offices had in place a decade or more ago for using foul language. Make your employees the decision makers.

✦ Provide plenty of positive reinforcement for the gains that have been made.

FAST STRATEGY #43

Know When to Raise the Standard Bar

ONE OF THE IMPORTANT RESPONSIBILITIES OF a coach is to develop competencies (FAST Strategy #31), and to know when and how to raise the standard bar. What are the signs that it's time to raise the standard bar?

♦ Employees' work is routinely completed with a high level of quality, long before deadline.

♦ Employees seem to be exhibiting symptoms of boredom with their current work assignments.

♦ Creativity seems to be stifled or nonexistent.

♦ Employees regularly (or even irregularly) ask for new tasks.

♦ Employees request professional development in areas that are more relevant to future assignments.

✦ The department or individual employees seem to be on "autopilot."

Raising the standard bar requires a great deal of judgment and finesse. Certainly you want employees to stretch to higher levels of achievement. However, you don't want them to stretch so much that it is counterproductive. To gently raise the standard bar, try these techniques:

✦ Raise the bar incrementally. Decide where the new standard should be and then identify three to five steps that will lead to the new standard. Work with each of the employees to reach the incremental steps.

✦ Set a deadline. There is great power in knowing that something must be done by a specific date. Develop a plan with the employees that allows each of them to reach the new standard by the stated deadline.

✦ Help each of the employees to raise his or her own standard bar. Coach them to self-identify the new standard. Work with them to decide when the standard should be kicked up a notch without prompting from you.

✦ Use If-then statements. For example, "If we are to cut expenses by 20 percent, then we will have to _____." Both you and the employees can mutually decide how to fill in the blank.

FAST STRATEGY #44

Use Failure as a Vehicle for Success

W<small>E ALL EXPERIENCE FAILURE DURING OUR</small> careers. In fact, it's said that success can only be born out of experiencing failure. Do the following statements sound familiar?

- Failed in business in 1831

- Defeated for Legislature in 1832

- Failed in business again in 1833

- Suffered nervous breakdown in 1836

- Defeated for Speaker in 1838

- Defeated for Elector in 1840

- Defeated for Congress in 1843

- Defeated for Congress in 1848

- Defeated for Senate in 1855

✦ Defeated for Vice President in 1856

✦ Defeated for Senate in 1858

✦ Elected President in 1860

The person who experienced these 11 failures was one of our greatest presidents, Abraham Lincoln. What if he had given up after his first failure, or even the second or third? Success does not come easily. What's important about our failures is that we learn from them.

It's especially critical to focus employees on what can be done to improve the next time. Morale can plummet, and employees may be hesitant to expose themselves to another failure. Managers can help employees work through failure by taking a positive stance.

Here are some suggestions:

✦ Debrief the employee after an unsuccessful project, meeting, or whatever was involved. Dissect each step of the project, looking at the actions that were taken at each step. Determine where the project went off track and what can be done in the future to prevent derailment.

✦ Look at the positive aspects of the project. Find something that is worthy of praise. Then ask the employee what he or she would change if the project could be done over.

✦ Use a force-field analysis to look at the forces that helped the project be successful and those that hindered project success. Analyze each, paying particular attention to those that were within the employee's control.

✦ Offer to assist the employee in mapping out the critical path of the next project. Identify checkpoints where you'll be available to discuss the project to ensure the work is on track.

✦ Offer reassurance and encouragement. Even one of our most beloved presidents had his share of personal and work-related failures. Success comes on the heels of failure. Encourage your employees to squarely face those failures and use them as learning points to reach higher levels of success.

FAST Strategy #45

Understand the Dynamics in the Organization

It's true. The new programs, changes, and improvements won't amount to much if they're squelched from above. Although your technical competency has, at least partially, gotten you to a management position, it's often understanding the intricacies of "how things work" at your organization that will make you a continued success.

Learning the dynamics of your organization can help you understand when and where to make your case. Here's what happened to one manager.

The weekly management meeting was often a quagmire of accusations and innuendo, and in fact, you never knew where the fickle finger of blame would point at any given moment. After one particularly brutal meeting (where a senior manager was ridiculed and severely chastised), our manager was overcome with a sense of rightness. She went to the CEO and said that she didn't want to be a part of a meeting that humiliated people. She explained that it just wasn't right and definitely not consistent with the culture that the organization was striving to create. The CEO listened to her thoughtfully and asked her if there was anything else she wanted to add. The manager said, "No," though she hoped the CEO understood where she was coming from. He replied that indeed he did, and he told her that she would not have to witness such behavior again. She thanked the CEO for his time and went back to her office, feeling as if a burden had been lifted from her highly ethical shoulders.

And lifted it was! That was the last meeting she went to for quite some time. It went something like this, "Since your boss is here, it's really not necessary to have both of you." This manager was learning to dance, but she stepped on too many seasoned toes, too early in the dance. Following the lead of the CEO, no one wanted to be her dance partner.

Although her position was one that was based in rightness and high ethical standards, she didn't understand the dynamics of the organization. Because of her ignorance, relationships with other departments were compromised and her own department staff suffered from the backlash.

A word on radar. Flying under the radar simply means getting the job done while massaging policy and procedure, but not enough to be scrutinized by upper management. I am not advocating deliberately going against policy and procedure. I am advocating having a thorough understanding so that you know how to massage the system. The alliances are the infrastructure built among employees at the company. It's an informal, underground system that keeps things moving and gets the job done. Even though its not on any organization chart, it's just as important.

To truly be in a position to effect changes in your department, you need to learn different dances, know how to fly under the radar, and solidify workplace alliances.

FAST STRATEGY #46

Give Employees Authority to Solve Problems

Aₙ OLD PIECE OF ADVICE THAT IS REGULARLY given to employees is, "Be a problem solver! Don't ever go to your boss with the problem—let him or her know how you have solved it or intend to solve it!" Sound advice . . . I think. Wouldn't it be great if employees effectively solved all their own problems and only came to you to let you know the solution and outcome? Fantasy, you say? Only in organizations that don't give authority to employees to solve the everyday problems that inevitably crop up.

The first step is to teach employees the basic problem-solving steps.

1. Define the problem exactly as it exists (no adjectives—they elicit unneeded emotion). Problem statements should not imply a solution. For example, "The monthly management staffing reports have been two weeks late for the past three months because the computer system

keeps going down." This immediately closes you off to potential solutions because it implies the computer system is at fault. This could be a potential cause, but without adequate data collection and information sharing, you can't be certain. You may also end up fixing a superfluous contributing cause, not the root cause of the problem. Writing a good problem statement is the most important step in the process.

2. Define what you see as the ideal state (what "it" will look like when the problem is solved). This will give you focus on where you're going and help in planning how you'll get there.

3. Write down the consequences, both positive and negative, that the problem has on your organization. This will help you focus and add validity as to whether or not this is a problem, and also give credence to the magnitude of the problem.

4. Determine possible root causes. Validate and reanalyze, using appropriate tools. Validate with data. This might mean postponing a decision until data can be gathered.

5. Determine if your original problem statement is still relevant considering the data that has been gathered.

6. Generate possible solutions. Use brainstorming techniques. Remember, nothing is too crazy or outside the box!

7. Select a possible solution. Ensure that there has been an objective analysis of the data.

8. Check to see if resources are available to implement the solution.

9. Determine how you will evaluate—how will you know that the solution has worked?

Educating your employees and mentoring them to become good problem solvers will help you be more effective in your job. If you want employees to become problem solvers, give them the tools to do it right.

FAST STRATEGY #47

Heat Up the Iron and Then Strike While It's Hot

Timing is everything . . . well, almost. Astute supervisors can sense when the timing is right for certain events, and then use this knowledge to their competitive advantage. Competitive advantage also includes improving the workplace environment. Strike while the iron's hot.

However, if the iron never gets hot, it can be difficult to heat it up yourself. Here are a few ways to build momentum:

1. Start small. Often it's hardest just to get started. If you can choose to start with issues or areas of lesser concern, it will be easier to achieve success. Save the big stuff for when you have a few successes under your belt. For example, you may want your employees to become more self-motivated (is there any other kind?). That is a worthy goal, but also a big one—difficult to

achieve and often the by-product of other environmental and management issues.

Maybe an employee has mentioned that a form should be redesigned or has an idea for better department coverage. Compared to motivation, these are fairly simple projects. They are very task-oriented. When someone is involved in a project that has clearly defined tasks, it's much easier to clearly see the successful outcome.

2. Make sure there is clear and public recognition on individual, departmental, and organizational bases.

3. Once you have a few successes under your belt (like the redesigned form or the department coverage), it's time to move to bigger and better things. It's time to strike while the iron's hot! Your employees will know how success feels, and since you've paid attention and been a part of the growth curve, they'll probably be more willing to undertake the bigger projects and issues.

This is by no means a guarantee that all will go as planned. There will be hurdles along the way. But, it's part of your job to remove the roadblocks that keep your employees from achieving higher levels of productivity and job satisfaction. Remember, this is a learning process and you must give employees the opportunity to do just that . . . learn.

FAST STRATEGY #48

Know Your Employees' Other Sides

Like Superman and Clark Kent, everyone has two sides. Ours may not be so drastically different, but certainly we have a work side and a personal side. Too often, supervisors only get to know the work side of a person. Not only does this prevent them from getting a well-rounded view of their employees, but it also cuts them off from information that might be critical in developing employees to their fullest potential.

We're told by misguided management gurus not to mix our employees' personal lives with business, but in following that advice we miss the boat on what may well be the most important information of all.

I'm not advocating cocktails every night after work—something a little more subtle works just as well. Try these conversation starters to help to get to know your staff better.

1. "How was your (weekend, vacation, bowling league, softball game . . . you get the picture)?"

2. "What do you do when you're not here slaving away?"

3. "What are your kids involved in?"

4. "I saw your (fill in the blank—son, daughter, spouse, cousin, etc.) in the paper. What he or she is doing sounds great! Tell me more about it."

5. "Let's grab a bite to eat—what's your favorite place to eat?"

6. "Those are great or that's a great (fill in the blank—shoes, slacks, pen, wall hanging, picture, vase, etc.). Where did you get it?"

These comments and questions aren't going to save the world. They may even seem simplistic, which begs the question, Why don't we engage in these types of conversations more often? Taking the first step to engage an employee in a non-work-related conversation opens up new possibilities. And by finding out what those new possibilities are, you may uncover a key to building an exceptional work environment.

FAST STRATEGY #49

Be Creative to Bring in the Best and Brightest

> *Creativity is thinking up new things.*
> *Innovation is doing new things.*
> —Theodore Levitt

MANY YEARS AGO, I WAS IN CHARGE OF recruiting manager trainees for a retail drugstore chain. It seemed that no matter how many advertisements we placed in the paper, how many job fairs we attended, or how many employee referrals we received, we always needed more trainees. We knew that we needed to step outside the box and come up with some creative approaches for recruiting or our competition would snap up all the "good ones." We needed a way to attract the best and brightest.

Competition? That got us thinking. Why only think about competition in negative terms? Instead of fearing the competition, why not figure out a way to use what they do well to our own competitive advantage? The seeds were planted!

It was evident that the larger variety stores had fairly extensive health and beauty aids (HBA) sections. Surely, an HBA manager might want to move up into his or her own store, rather than continuing to work under a large store manager. I began to walk through the HBA sections. If the department looked good, I'd ask for the HBA manager and compliment him or her on how nice the section looked. (I was specific . . . "the shelves are well-stocked" or "the floors look great—someone really knows how to run a buffer!") This may not seem like a big thing, but in actuality, it was the deal maker! You see, the only time someone commented on the HBA section was when the district manager was yelling at the HBA manager. The compliments went a long way. I'd also discreetly hand my card over and say, "If you know anyone looking for a manager trainee position with the intention of moving into his or her own store within a year, please tell that person to give me a call." Needless to say, the phone would ring!

What did I know about my competition? I knew that they had a reputation for hiring top-notch people. My competitor was large enough to offer pay and benefits that I could not offer up front. However, I also knew that my competition had a slow-moving career path and that advancement meant moving far away. Store managers had a typical tenure of 10 to 15 years . . . far too long for a high-potential department manager to wait. Most of these department managers had a local family and did not want to move. Our organization was able to use all of these factors to our competitive advantage, and in the long run attracted the best and brightest manager trainees.

FAST STRATEGY #50

Understand Your Own Weaknesses

Sometimes we're hesitant to use "hard" words. The word *weakness* has been replaced by *developmental need*. However, it's our own weakness that blinds us to what truly needs to be done to build an exceptional workplace environment.

In *The Five Temptations of a CEO*, author Patrick Lencioni tells in a narrative fashion why CEOs fail. Although this is written with the CEO in mind, its learning points can be used by anyone in a management position. The five temptations come down to poor choices. In short, they are:

1. Choosing status over results

2. Choosing popularity over accountability

3. Choosing certainty over clarity

4. Choosing harmony over productive conflict

5. Choosing invulnerability over trust

As managers, we make these choices, and when the former is chosen over the latter, our employees suffer. When faced with these hard choices, it's important to think in the long term. Poor choices come from a short-term, self-promoting focus. To avoid yielding to the temptations, it's important to have upward communication. Managers need to have a conduit for information that employees can offer, anonymously if needed. It's also important to be willing to take a hard look at how these temptations affect us.

Avoiding these five downfalls requires forethought and a mindset of continuous improvement. Ask yourself these questions:

1. Do I put more emphasis on my position in the organization than on the long-term well-being of the organization as a whole?

2. Am I willing to ask my employees tough questions and hold them accountable for their answers?

3. Do I put off decision making because I'm afraid of being wrong, or do I focus on clarifying information so that I can make decisions quickly and confidently?

4. Do I seek out diverse opinions from my department or team and facilitate discussion where all opinions are valued?

5. Am I willing to admit (to others) when I'm wrong, or do I enter a "spin zone" that justifies my position?

The answers to these questions will give you some clarity on whether or not you're yielding to the temptations. Better yet, let your employees respond anonymously to these questions. The answers you get may be surprising. But, the true surprise comes when you make changes and see a noticeable workplace improvement.

FAST STRATEGY #51

Treat Your Employees Like Customers

Customers frequently get our best, and whatever is left over goes to our employees. Employees are really our customers, too. They are our internal customers and are as important to our core business as the external, or paying, customers.

If we applied the principles of customer loyalty to employee loyalty, we just might see a decrease in turnover and an increase in motivation and loyalty. There are four significant factors of building and maintaining loyalty.

1. The Build, Cement, or Destroy Factor

Every interaction you have with employees (your internal customers) has the potential to either build, cement, or destroy the relationship. Customers and employees want relationships based on authenticity and trust. When we don't try to make them understand us, we violate that trust. When we don't deal with them authentically, we violate that trust.

It is all about communication. I don't just mean verbal communication. There are many ways to communicate, including e-mail, fax, and teleconference. Choose your words and presentation formats to make your employees most comfortable. Our buzz-words may not be theirs, especially for newer employees, and may even make them uncomfortable or put them in an underdog position. Efforts to dazzle can blind.

2. The Potentially Most Important Resource: People

In this day of massive meltdowns and layoffs, mergers and acquisitions, the emphasis on people is all the more critical. Why are people so important? Because the personal relationship is still at the core of the customer relationship. Employees want to work with people who they believe are genuinely interested in them, who speak their language, and who seem to have a vested interest in their success.

Don't be afraid to put your money—your budget —where your mouth is. Resources for development are critical to a healthy organization. Try to keep the flames alive once the development spark has been lit. It's a lot like romance: dating, marriage, honeymoon, and then the day to day. Keep that romantic spark! After all, if you're not romancing your employees day in, day out, year in, year out, someone else will!

3. Touchy or Techie

The most successful companies will effectively meld "high tech" with "high touch." Technology doesn't necessarily give us more free time, does it? Use it carefully and understand your metrics. Use metrics to lend clarity and track employee behavior, and to improve employee loyalty and retention. How can you use this to better understand your employees as human beings rather than as objects or commodities?

Even with the advantages that technology brings, employees still need a face-to-face or voice-to-voice relationship. Employees want to be able to take advantage of all the bells and whistles that high tech brings, but they also need a human hand to walk them through it.

4. The Button It Up and Sew It On Phenomenon

Our family routinely uses Dewitt Cleaners. They are not the cheapest and definitely not the closest dry cleaners to our home. What makes Dewitt Cleaners stand out is the fact that I notice the differences and truly appreciate them. What are the differences? It's the buttons and seams. If a shirt is missing a button, they sew it on. If a pair of pants has a ripped seam, they sew it up. They do this without being asked. They usually let us know when the cleaning is picked up that it's been done, at no charge. This is what makes a difference; this is what is appreciated.

Ask your employees what is it that you do that makes a difference to them. What do they truly appreciate? Then use that to build loyalty.

Here's the question: "In your last experience or interaction with me, what was most memorable?" That's right, memorable. The answer to that question, or lack thereof, will help you help your internal customers recognize and appreciate your differences and build loyalty.

FAST Strategy #52

Know How to Sustain Improvements

YOU'RE SITTING IN A STAFF MEETING. SOME-one brings up the topic of improving organizational communications. Everyone is in agreement that communication is definitely something that needs improvement. As all heads are nodding in the affirmative, someone says, "Yeah . . . but we did a training on communication last year, and it didn't help!"

Think about how many new processes you've implemented that have fallen by the wayside or training that's been attended that was forgotten a week later. What happened? Perhaps it wasn't relevant or useful. Most likely there was no mechanism in place to sustain a long-term change. Use the SUSTAIN acronym:

Systematic

Understanding

Small Piece Plans

Tolerance

Accountability

Investment Mentality

Navigate

Systematic

To ensure that the changes you've put into place stick, it's important to have a systematic plan in place. The plan should outline what needs to happen, who needs to do it, time lines, and expected results. Review the plan regularly (once a week or so) with the relevant players, and tweak as necessary. You also need a systematic way to communicate, make changes, provide resources, and address issues and conflicts as they arise. Leaving these items to chance is risking failure.

The most direct path between two points may be a straight line, but it's highly unlikely that will be the path you take. Anticipate potholes, roadblocks, and other detours. Road hazards come from all directions—employees, managers, the organization, customers, and you. Learn to be flexible and to entertain more than one way of going from Point A to Point B. Be prepared to use contingency plans, because we all know that "the best laid plans . . . ."

Understanding

Your understanding:

✦ Do you understand the situation as it exists? The desired state?

✦ Do you understand the resources that will be needed?

✦ Do you understand your employees' skill sets and what they will need to implement and sustain the change?

✦ Do you understand the employees' perceptions of their work environment and the impact of this change?

Employees' understanding:

✦ Do employees fully understand the situation?

✦ Has there been any level of involvement up to the present?

✦ What communication systems are in place to promote employee understanding?

Organizational understanding:

✦ Do the "powers-that-be" understand how this change will impact and improve your department or team?

✦ Is there support, both in words and resources, for you?

Small Piece Plans

The rest of the business world does not stop while you're trying to build and sustain an exceptional workplace environment. There may be other projects and work assignments that take your time. There may be constant fires to put out. There are many reasons why time constraints prevent us from carrying out this program.

Your intentions are good, but sometimes . . .

That's why it's important to develop a plan that can be implemented on a piece-by-piece basis. It's very similar to the old adage about eating an elephant—one bite at a time!

If you're fortunate enough to be able to implement everything at once, great! But for most of us, it's on a piece-by-piece basis. Use realistic scheduling tools and significant checkpoints.

Tolerance

Tolerance is not only for the people with whom you're working, but also for yourself. You will stumble. Your people will stumble. You may try new techniques and not get the expected results. Your people will become frustrated because "it takes too long." You, too, may become frustrated.

This is an evolutionary process. We are all human and, as with any change, it takes time and practice to fully integrate a new way of doing something. Cut yourself and the people who report to you some slack. A word of caution, however. Don't cut so much slack that you lower the standard bar or deviate from the path that will help you attain your goals.

Accountability

The buck stops with you. You are in charge. The success or lack of success is solely upon you. You are the manager or supervisor and therefore you have the power to ensure that changes are made where they are most needed. If you don't have that power, think twice about implementing something new. Power, authority, and accountability. All incredibly energizing when properly channeled.

Do you have employees who don't want to get with the program? It's up to you to get them there. What standards you set and expect people to reach are almost totally dependent on you. Nothing will change if you aren't leading the change. Don't have the time? Then don't expect anyone else to have time, either. The fact is, you don't have the time *not* to develop and coach your people and demand accountability. You can always go back to the good old days . . . and spend those days playing catch-up.

Investment Mentality

Merriam-Webster's Collegiate Online Dictionary defines *investment* as "the outlay of money usually for income or profit: capital outlay." The word *investment* implies a risk factor. As a manager, the outlay of money comes in the form of hiring and turnover costs. The profit, of course, is a high-performing employee, which takes time. Anyone who went through the roller coaster ride of the 2001 stock market knows that short-term investing can be disastrous. It's a long-term, strategic view that nets the highest profits. When investing in employees, look at the long-term goals and be willing to effectively deal with the highs and lows that often accompany a learning curve.

Navigate

Prepare for the next level. Always anticipate where you and your employees need to be, and be prepared to move there at a moment's notice. Build momentum and be able to strike while the iron's hot (FAST Strategy #47). Know how to effectively navigate within your organization so that you can lead your employees to achieving their goals. Teach your employees to navigate themselves by clearly communicating goals and mentoring them during the process.

APPENDIX A

Implementing FAST 52 Strategies— The Process Model

Successfully implementing FAST 52 strategies is best illustrated with the FAST 52 Process Model. The model is a dynamic and fluid infrastructure and is based on a combination of five elements:

✦ Long-term goals

✦ Communication

✦ Ownership

◆ Metrics and milestones

◆ Reward and recognition

Three elements—long-term goals, communication, and ownership—provide the outer framework for the model. The elements are interdependent; that is, one cannot successfully exist without the other. Metrics and milestones and reward and recognition form the internal infrastructure of the model. This is what sustains the process and holds the framework together. All elements logically flow back and forth; that is, there is a constant exchange of information between and among the elements.

Long-term Goals

Long-term goals are what you're striving to accomplish through implementing FAST 52 strategies. It goes without saying that you want to build a better work environment. Your long-term goal can be as simple as "build a happier, more productive team." All actions flow from the long-term goals. The goals are often derived from the strategic plan or business plan, vision, or mission statement. Long-term goals should have the following characteristics:

1. They should be stated in clear, understandable language. Avoid jargon, acronyms, and other confusing language.

2. They should be tangible and far-reaching. Employees need to mentally touch the goals and understand that those goals are part of a

bigger picture. Employees need to understand how their work aids in attainment of the goal.

3. They should have stretch. Make the goal a result of a significant effort. Goals that are too easily accomplished lose meaning and may very well not be goals at all, but rather a means to a goal.

4. Daily actions should directly relate to the long-term goal at hand. Don't be afraid to tell people what you're doing. If you don't, it's very likely that your staff won't notice. You must let them know what you're doing and then follow up to gauge the effect.

Long-term goals are built on a foundation of communication and ownership.

Communication

A vibrant communication system must be in place in order for the goals to stand and be acted upon. An effective communication system possesses the following characteristics:

1. It flows in three directions—from the lowest employee level to the highest management level (bottom-up); from the highest management level to the lowest employee level (top-down); and inside and outside departments and functional groups (laterally).

2. It is rooted in trust and respect. Those engaged in the communication process hold each other's opinions, comments, and information in high

regard. This does not necessarily mean that there is agreement, but it does mean that there is mutual support.

3. It possesses a high level of productive conflict. People feel comfortable in speaking their minds, even if it means a disagreement will ensue. However, all parties have well-honed conflict management skills enabling them to synthesize the information and arrive at a reasonable outcome.

Ownership

Ownership refers to the commitment that any given person has toward the process in which he or she is engaged. It is through ownership that individuals have a stake in the outcome of the process. They are physically and mentally absorbed and have more than just a personal interest in seeing a successful outcome. People with a high degree of ownership exhibit the following characteristics:

1. They have internalized the goal and feel a sense of personal responsibility for achieving that goal. Without a high-functioning communication system, this can be perceived as territoriality, so both parts of this foundation must go hand-in-hand.

2. Their task-related actions are designed to help reach the goal. In fact, many of these people have well-developed prioritization and delegation skills.

3. They feel a sense of ownership and are talkative regarding what they own. It forms a basis of peer and supervisory relationships, and becomes a bonding agent.

Metrics and milestones and reward and recognition are what feed and sustain the process.

Metrics and Milestones

Establishing metrics and milestones is a twofold process. First, establish two types of metrics: long-term and intermediary. The long-term metric is directly tied to achieving the overarching goal and may be expressed in a variety of ways. For example:

1. Reduce turnover by 20 percent.

2. Eliminate employee complaints regarding . . .

3. Increase patient satisfaction scores to 95 percent.

4. Increase employee opinion survey scores to 4.5.

Notice that all of these are expressed in some type of quantitative form. Even the goal that states, "Eliminate employee complaints regarding . . ." is quantitative because it refers to going from some number to zero. Be careful of how you express the metric. If it's expressed in the form of "Increase employee opinion survey scores" or something similar but doesn't include a goal number, you won't have a shared sense of what success means.

The milestones are the intermediary goals. If you're trying to reduce turnover by 20 percent, the plan you develop might look something like this:

MILESTONE OR INTERMEDIARY GOAL	ACTION NEEDED	PEOPLE RESPONSIBLE	DONE BY
Determine root cause(s) of turnover.	Form a vertically cut committee that will gather and analyze existing data from: • Exit interviews • Employee opinion surveys • Focus groups.	HR director	March 15
Make recommendations on where to focus efforts based on data analysis.	Prepare committee recommendations based on resource availability.	Committee chairperson	April 5
Present draft plan to management for approval.	Develop specific step-by-step plan that includes action items and resources needed, such as people, equipment, time, and budget. This should also include an ROI analysis.	Committee person—TBD	May 1
If approved: Implement. If not approved: Redo with necessary changes.	Develop communications for organization and gain needed buy-in. Go back to committee for revised draft plan based on needed changes.	HR director and committee chairperson Committee chairperson	May 15
Monitor plan and evaluate effectiveness.	Develop and implement a mechanism for evaluating success.	Committee person—TBD	May 15 and ongoing
Assess success and continue or make changes as needed.	Prepare committee analysis of success factors.	Committee chairperson	Ongoing, at quarterly intervals

Reward and Recognition

Reward and recognition systems are an outgrowth of achieving milestones. It's important to remember to recognize people for effort and reward for results. When you have established concrete milestones, as in the previous table, it's easy to reward and recognize people in a timely way. In this example, you might want to recognize people for the effort and hard work that they've put into analyzing the data. Be specific in recognizing each individual for the distinct skill set brought to the table. One person may have great attention to detail, while another person is able to assimilate vastly different data sets. And yet another person may have an uncanny knack of seeing both sides of an issue or bringing clarity to issues that seem to have none. While an "atta boy" is always good, make it more meaningful by specifying just why that person is getting recognized.

Reward, on the other hand, is something a little more tangible. You may decide that when management approves the draft plan you'll have some sort of celebration. Or, you could even tell people to knock off work early on a Friday afternoon. Another way to reward is to present the team with some sort of certificate, pin, or other token that specifically says they were an integral part of a successful team. The possibilities are limited only by your imagination (and perhaps budget). Each person values different things; make sure you know what's important to each individual and then use it.

There is synergy among and between the model's components. They nourish each other and provide a

sustainable framework for success. The success of the FAST 52 Process Model lies in the interdependency of the components. While you would make progress focusing on any one part of the model, true, sustainable results derive from embracing the model as a whole. When each component of the model is used in harmony, you can expect to achieve far greater results than if you had used any part or parts of the model alone.

Each component flows in two directions. Beginning with the framework—Long-term goals, communication, and ownership—you'll notice an almost automatic flow and exchange of information and action among the three components. Establishing long-term goals that are meaningful and understood by all requires you to put into place a comprehensive communication system. That communication system further reinforces the long-term goals. At the same time, driving down the long-term goals provides the opportunity for ownership of the goals, which in turn fosters more commitment toward achieving the goals. Concurrently, owning those goals sparks communication, and in turn, more communication about goals encourages people to take a more involved role. When this dynamic occurs, you have a framework that has both strength and flexibility, is both solid and fluid, and becomes sustained by both management and employees.

While long-term goals, communication, and ownership would seem to be enough, it is only a good start. Without metrics and milestones and reward and recognition, the model can spiral into a long and painful death. These two components provide the nourishment to energize and feed each person in the process.

Metrics and milestones are critical because people naturally do better when they know what they're supposed to achieve and how they're progressing. Seems simple, but it is often a neglected part of the workplace environment. Most employees only know their metrics in very vague terms. Until they get the annual performance appraisal, it's just not in the forefront of their minds and by then it's too late. Most employees will tell you they don't refer to that appraisal very often during the year, and unless they're involved in an intensive project, there is very little done in terms of establishing metrics or milestones.

Using metrics and milestones allows you to easily lead your team in the right direction. Two important characteristics of high-performing teams are that they move as one and are singularly focused on a shared goal. A team must know what's expected of them and how they'll be measured for success. Instituting metrics and milestones gives each person clear direction on the who, what, where, when, and why of what needs to be accomplished.

Reward and recognition systems reinforce both the energy and expertise that people put into their work and the corresponding results. When the reward and recognition flows from the metrics and milestones, people are more likely to continue to achieve based on the positive reinforcement. It is truly a two-way street. Work hard and get recognized. Reach a milestone, get rewarded. Get rewarded and be more likely to want to reach the next milestone. Work hard to reach the milestone and get more recognition. Get more recognition and successfully reach the next milestone. And so the cycle goes.

One cannot exist for any length of time without the other. The metrics and milestones are what make the reward and recognition meaningful. They also set an expectation that if certain criteria are met, then certain positive reinforcement will occur. It is truly a case of cause and effect and adds the fuel that boosts ownership and communication and attainment of the long-term goal.

Maria's Story

Maria is a 51-year-old manager in a manufacturing setting. She has 21 employees reporting to her, most with 5 to 10 years of service. The group is made up equally of males and females, and the age range is 21 to 55 years. Maria has worked for the organization for 18 years and has been in her current supervisory position for the last 4 years.

Most days, Maria thinks she is a glorified baby-sitter. She is continuously checking up on staff to make sure they are at their workstations on time and work the entire shift. Some have a tendency to take off 5 or 10 minutes early. Productivity just barely meets the standard. This bothers Maria, because she suspects that if people would spend less time engaged in idle chitchat and more time engaged in work, productivity would increase dramatically.

Lately, Maria has noticed complaining and commiserating taking a strong foothold in the group. Even employees normally exempt from this type of behavior have fallen victim. Morale is falling, and there seems to be no end in sight. Maria has tried team meetings, praising people, and even having pizza parties (out of her own money), but there doesn't seem to be any lasting impact.

When Maria came to me, she was out of ideas and seriously considering firing the majority of her staff and starting again with new people. Using the FAST 52 Model, we began to identify ways that she could energize and invigorate not only her staff, but also herself.

Maria's long-term goal was to increase productivity and decrease morale problems. When asked how morale problems manifested in the group, it became clear that it was mostly through employees' sniping comments about who wasn't pulling his or her weight in the group. Maria agreed that it was nearly impossible to eliminate all employee complaining. What she really wanted was to have employees work out problems with each other in an open, honest, and respectful way. Maria was unclear, though, on what type of increase in productivity she wanted. After about one-half hour of discussion, she decided to play it safe and go for a 10 percent increase in productivity.

Maria's long-term goal is to increase productivity by 10 percent. Eliminate the underhanded, behind-the-back employee complaints about each other by encouraging employees to work out issues together. (This is directly tied to part of the organization's mission and two key result areas.)

While eliminating the behind-the-back employee complaints seemed a little lofty, Maria strongly felt that there was no compromise on this issue.

With the long-term goal in place, we began to focus on the communication systems. Communication was primarily top-down and done through staff meetings and written memos. The staff meetings usually took about one-half hour and were scheduled for the beginning of the shift, every other Tuesday. The typical agenda at the staff meeting consisted of policy changes, new orders, review of previous two-week production, safety, and miscellaneous items. Maria chaired the meetings and relayed most of the information. The bottom-up communication occurred almost exclusively when there was a problem. As we know, lateral communications took the form of complaints.

Because there was already a structure in place for staff meetings, we felt that this would be a good place to start building the communication foundation. Maria also committed to having more one-on-one conversations with people. This would serve two purposes. First, it allowed her to get to know her people as individuals and build better relationships. Secondly, it would allow her to become aware of problems when they were still at a manageable level.

For the staff meeting component, Maria implemented two strategies: FAST Strategy #33, Establish Goals and Have Frequent Goal Meetings, and FAST

Strategy #35, Conduct Effective Department and Team Meetings. She changed the frequency of staff meetings to every week. She also changed the format to be more goal oriented and used the SMART (Specific, Measurable, Attainable or Action-Oriented, Relevant or Realistic, Timely) goal formula. Agendas were prepared ahead of time, and she solicited input from staff for agenda items. She got staff involved in meetings by having them participate in the roles of timekeeper and recorder. Action items were established at every meeting, and the meetings strictly adhered to a results orientation.

Tackling the one-on-one interactions was a little more challenging. Since Maria had not previously engaged in these types of conversations, she was concerned that it would come off as disingenuous or phony. To attack this issue head-on, Maria called a 15-minute meeting with her department to explain what she was going to do.

With her group sitting in a semicircle, she took a deep breath and began, "I want to first let you know that as a group we have the potential to do great things. While we're doing okay now, I think that we can reach even higher levels of achievement." Maria looked around to gauge the group. In some eyes, she saw confusion. But mostly, she saw polite boredom. She continued, "I want you to know that I believe in our group, and that's why I'm so eager to move ahead. Everyone on this team, myself included, will probably have to do some things differently. That can be difficult, so it's important that we all support one another. One of the things I'll be doing is talking more with all of you on a one-on-one basis. That may seem a little out of character for me, but I think it's important, so bear with me. (*Maria could swear she saw at least six sets of eyes roll!*) You'll also be seeing some changes in how we have staff meetings, so if you have questions or concerns, please let me know."

As the employees got up to leave, Maria noticed that they were considerably more quiet than usual. She didn't know what to make of it and hoped it was a good sign.

Getting started on the individual conversations was easier than Maria thought. Using FAST Strategy #22, Communicate for Understanding, and FAST Strategy #48, Know Your Employees' Other Sides, Maria found that initiating and sustaining conversations was not only beneficial, but also enjoyable. She found out things about her employees that she never knew before. Michael's daughter had just been inducted into the National Honor Society, and Fran had participated in a walk-a-thon that raised more than $30,000. She found out Julian read to elementary school children once a month and Morgan was entering a chili cook-off. John went to the dirt bike track every weekend, and at least three other employees were there to cheer him on. It became clear to her that each employee was involved in interesting things outside of work. What was even clearer was all that energy and enthusiasm disappeared once they punched in for the shift. She made a mental note to think about how to tap into all that energy.

Ownership was a trickier nut to crack. After all, how can you force people to take ownership of something in which they appear to have little or no interest? The answer lies in turning the tables. I posed the following questions to Maria. "From your employees' perspectives, what is the value in taking ownership of this process? What will they get out of it? Why is it in their best interest? And finally, what's the WIIFM (What's in it for me) factor?"

After about 15 minutes of brainstorming, Maria had come up with the following concise answers:

✦ They will have an opportunity to really use their knowledge and skills to make a difference. They gripe about how people who make the rules and tell them how to work don't understand the job they do. This will address the issue and give them more ownership of the process.

✦ It will allow a positive exchange of ideas and fresh perspectives.

✦ They will be able to see a recommendation or idea through from start to finish. The success or failure will depend on them.

Maria decided to introduce the idea of ownership and also communicate the long-term goal at the next staff meeting. She would start with FAST Strategy #3, Ask for Your Employees' Recommendations on Job-Related Problems, and FAST Strategy #37, Help Employees Develop a "Big Picture" Focus. The problem she decided to focus on was tardiness and employees repeatedly leaving the shift 5 or 10 minutes early. Maria also decided to throw in unscheduled absenteeism, as that was also becoming an issue. If these issues could be resolved, the road would be cleared for reaching the long-term goal.

What happened at that staff meeting was not at all what Maria was anticipating. She thought that people would politely nod but not say much. Just the opposite was true. Employees were very vocal about their feelings on the subject. It was apparent that this issue was a sore spot with most people. What came next was completely unexpected.

There was a steady stream of negativity, and while all true, it was not productive in terms of getting the group to take ownership and solve the problem. Trying to lend structure to the process, Maria turned to FAST Strategy #42, Find the Jewel (When Clouds Are Dark). Maria summarized all the comments on a flip chart and then said, "We have quite a list of things here. What we need to do is figure out a way to solve the problems of coming in late, leaving early, and not coming in at all. Now, I'd like to hear your suggestions, so take a minute or two to gather your thoughts, and then let's go around the group so everyone's idea can be heard."

At that point, one of the employees, Janice, stood up and said, "I think we have another problem that we should work on. It's all the negativity. People here say more negative things than positive things, and we ought to do something about that, too."

Maria thanked Janice and asked, "Group, what do you think? Is this something we should work on?" As she looked around, almost every person was either saying yes or nodding in agreement. "Okay then, let's add this on, too."

Not one to let an opportunity like this slide by, Maria asked the group to "get it all out." She went to each person, in round-robin fashion, and asked them to contribute something related to the negativity. After several times around the circle, the group had come up with three flip chart pages of negative comments. Looking at it was almost a defining moment for the group, and Mark offered, "Gee, I hope this gets it out for everyone!"

Maria looked around but was having a difficult time reading the group. Rather than commenting, she moved back to the original notion of taking everyone's suggestions to deal with the issues at hand.

After all the ideas were put up on a flip chart, Maria asked the group to vote on which ideas they liked best for solving the problems. Overwhelming, the group decided the following:

1. People saying negative things would get fined 25 cents. It would go into a jar in Maria's office. At the end of the month, any money in the jar would go toward getting pizza for lunch. Maria, knowing that she wanted less quarters, not more quarters, said that if the jar was short money at the end of the month, she would buy pizza, and would continue buying it every

month. Little did she realize what a motivator this would become!

2. To handle the tardiness, early departures, and unscheduled or unexcused absenteeism, the employees asked Maria to post everyone's name on a white board by her office. Each day, she would record the previous day's activity. This would be addressed at the staff meeting, now being held on a weekly basis. The group was adamant that they, not Maria, should deal with this. Maria hesitantly conceded and decided to take a wait and see approach. The group affectionately named these the "You're not here sheets."

The meeting ended with Maria reiterating the long-term goal and summing up the major points and action items from the meeting. As the meeting broke up, Maria could hear giggles and see smiles on almost everyone. She did hear two people comment that they were going to go out and buy a couple of rolls of quarters to cover their negative comments.

With the long-term goal, communication, and ownership components in place, Maria moved to the next phase. Establishing metrics and milestones easily fell into place. Maria went back to the long-term goal to increase productivity by 10 percent and eliminate the underhanded, behind-the-back employee complaints about one another. It was critical to continuously connect all of her actions toward accomplishing the long-term goal. Using the group's idea of the quarter jar, she decided to announce how much money was in the jar each week, perhaps even more often in the beginning. The idea of posting everyone's attendance on the white board was modified somewhat and posted on a spreadsheet. Each week's spreadsheet was kept up on the board so everyone could view the activity at any given time. Only unexcused absences, tardiness, and early departures were posted. Maria coordinated with the human resources department to make sure that everything was compliant with state, local, and federal regulations.

Reward and recognition also seemed to easily follow. Now that she was talking regularly with employees on an informal, one-on-one basis, meaningful praise seemed to flow. Her conversations eventually turned to, "What motivates you?" (FAST Strategy #15, Find Out What Motivates Employees, and Then Use It). The information she gleaned from these conversations became the keystone for rewarding and recognizing employees. As employees began to get more positive, meaningful reinforcement, they became more vocal about their jobs and how they'd like to do some things differently. Maria jumped on this and quickly made use of FAST Strategy #41, Look for Opportunities to Develop Employees' Skills.

The Quarter Jar

A very large glass jar was located to accommodate the anticipated high volume of negativity quarters. At the end of day 1, there was $4.25 worth of quarters.

The end of day 2 saw $4.75. At the beginning of day 3, Maria shuddered. At this rate, she'd be able to buy pizza in a week! She posted the first two days' results on the white board and went about her day. The next morning she counted the quarters and smiled—$3.00. She posted the results. The next day $2.25. Again, she posted the results. With the exception of three "blips," after the first week each day averaged anywhere from zero quarters to $0.75. In Maria's mind, this was nothing short of a miracle. In the minds of her employees, this was just another challenge to be conquered.

It was not surprising that Maria got happily stuck chipping in for pizza that month. There just weren't enough quarters to cover it for everyone. After another three months of buying pizza out of her own money, the employees told her that they didn't want her to do it anymore—that they should all chip in. Maria agreed but still keeps the quarter jar in full view.

The You're Not Here Sheets

If Maria had not been a part of this, she would not have believed the outcome. The first morning, Morgan, Julian, and Mark came to her door asking, "Where are the sheets?" Maria looked up and said, "I haven't even gotten to them yet. Give me some time." Mark stepped forward a bit and said, "If this is going to work, you have to get these up first thing in the morning. It won't work if we can't see them when we first get here."

Maria thought *talk about turnabout. Well, I guess I better be on top of this.*

"Okay, I'll get them up right away. Give me 10 minutes." Maria was watching the three walk away when Mark turned and walked back to the office. "Maria, most of us are on board with this. But you probably have figured out that the people who aren't on board are the people with the biggest attendance problems. If you wait to do this, no one will think you're serious, especially the problem people. Believe me, there's a bunch of us who are tired of carrying other people's workload."

Maria thanked Mark for his comments and wondered if this really could make a difference. Four weeks later she knew.

On a Wednesday morning, Maria came into her office early to review the attendance sheets. She wanted to have them up before the shift came in. She had seen small improvements here and there, but nothing consistent. After she finished the "You're Not Here Sheet," she smiled. No late arrivals. No early departures. No unscheduled absences. She posted the sheet outside her office and waited for the shift to arrive.

By the hooting and hollering, Maria knew the news was out. Then an interesting thing happened. She heard employees complimenting other employees for their dedication in having a perfect sheet. That was the turning point, and after that perfect sheets became the norm rather than the exception.

The Goal

It was now four months since Maria had started using the FAST 52 Process Model and integrating FAST 52 strategies into her management style. The negative comments were almost nonexistent. People came to work on time and left on time, ready to tackle whatever issues were thrown their way. She rarely had to deal with employee-to-employee issues anymore, as the group was working out concerns among themselves. Mark and Janice had stepped into informal team leader roles and were instrumental in keeping things running smoothly. Although their styles were very different, they both had developed trust with their coworkers and people outside the department. Maria regularly walked the shop floor, stopping for informal conversations with as many people as possible.

The best news of all came a week later. The quarterly production numbers were looking good. Although productivity was not up 10 percent, it was showing a 4 percent increase and that was a good sign. Maria knew it would take 9 to 12 months to reach the 10 percent figure. Sharing this news with the group only got them more excited and more determined than ever to reach and exceed the 10 percent productivity increase.

Maria reflected back on the goal: Increase productivity by 10 percent. Eliminate the underhanded, behind-the-back employee complaints about one another by encouraging employees to work out issues with one another. Four months ago, she would not have thought it possible to reach this. She remembered being on the verge of firing everyone and starting with new people. At this point she realized that perhaps the problem wasn't with her staff, it was with her methods. And now she understood how to tap into the energy her employees previously reserved for outside interests.

Firmly resolved to never let the work environment return to its former state, Maria looked to her next round of FAST 52 strategies. Speaking aloud she quietly said, "Hmmm . . . this one looks good. FAST Strategy #51, Treat Your Employees Like Customers. And this is one I definitely need to do, FAST Strategy #52, Know How to Sustain Improvements." She looked at the clock, and it was almost 5:00 p.m. Although tomorrow would bring new challenges and perhaps a few old ones that wouldn't go away, Maria knew that she and her employees were well equipped to handle anything thrown their way.

APPENDIX B

52 Resources
for a Better Workplace

The following is by no means a comprehensive listing of resource reading; however, it's a good start, and you may just find one or two books to help you on your FAST 52 journey.

Ahlrichs, Nancy S. *Competing for Talent: Key Recruitment and Retention Strategies for Becoming an Employer of Choice*. Palo Alto, CA: Davies-Black Publishing, 2001.

Barbazette, Jean. *Successful New-Employee Orientation: Assess, Plan and Evaluate Your Program with CD-ROM*. San Francisco, CA: Jossey-Bass Publishers, Inc., 2001.

Barner, Robert W. *Team Troubleshooter: How to Find and Fix Team Problems*. Palo Alto, CA: Davies-Black Publishing, 2001.

Blanchard, Kenneth, et al. *High Five: The Magic of Working Together*. New York, NY: William Morrow & Co., 2000.

Branham, F. Leigh. *Keeping the People Who Keep You in Business: 24 Ways to Hang on to Your Most Valuable Talent*. New York, NY: AMACOM, 2000.

Bruce, Anne, and James S. Pepitone. *Motivating Employees*. New York, NY: McGraw-Hill Professional, 1998.

Buckingham, Marcus, and Curt Coffman. *First, Break All the Rules: What the World's Greatest Managers Do Differently*. New York, NY: Simon & Schuster, 1999.

Catlette, Bill, and Richard Hadden. *Contented Cows Give Better Milk*. Germantown, TN: Williford Communications, 2000.

Charan, Ram, Stephen Drotter, and James Noel. *The Leadership Pipeline: How to Build the Leadership Powered Company*. San Francisco, CA: Jossey-Bass Publishers, Inc., 2000.

Cohen, David S. *The Talent Edge: A Behavioral Approach to Hiring, Developing and Keeping Top Performers*. New York, NY: John Wiley & Sons, Inc., 2001.

Cohen, Dr. Norman H. *A Step-By-Step Guide to Starting an Effective Mentoring Program*. Amherst, MA: Human Resource Development Press, 2000.

Collins, James. *Good to Great: Why Some Companies Make the Leap . . . And Others Don't*. New York, NY: HarperCollins Publishers, 2001.

Covey, Stephen R. *The 7 Habits of Highly Effective People*. New York, NY: Simon & Schuster, 1989.

Crandall, Rick. *Break-Out Creativity: Bringing Creativity to the Workplace*. Corte Madera, CA: Select Press, 1997.

Crane, Thomas, Larissa Nancy Parker, and Troy S. Parker (Illustrator). *The Heart of Coaching: Using Transformational Coaching to Create a High Performance Culture*, rev. ed. Ronkonkoma, NY: FTA Press, 2001.

Daniels, Aubrey C. *Bringing Out the Best in People.* New York, NY: McGraw-Hill Professional, 1999.

Deblieux, Mike. *Supervisor's Guide to Employee Performance Reviews.* Charlottesville, VA: LEXIS Publishing, 1999.

Elton, Chester, and Adrian Robert Gostick. *Managing with Carrots: Using Recognition to Attract and Retain the Best People.* Salt Lake City, UT: Gibbs Smith, 2001.

Goleman, Daniel. *Emotional Intelligence.* New York, NY: Bantam Books, 1995, 1997.

Hacker, Carol A. *How to Compete in the War for Talent: A Guide to Hiring the Best.* Sanford, FL: Douglas Charles, Limited, 2001.

Herman, Roger E. *Keeping Good People: Strategies for Solving the #1 Problem Facing Business Today.* Winchester, VA: OakHill Press, 1998.

Huszczo, Gregory E. *Tools for Team Excellence: Getting Your Team Into High Gear and Keeping It There.* Palo Alto, CA: Davies-Black Publishing, 1996.

Johnson, Spencer, and Kenneth Blanchard. *Who Moved My Cheese? An Amazing Way to Deal with Change in Your Work and in Your Life.* New York, NY: The Putnam Publishing Group, 1998.

Juran, J. M. *Managerial Breakthrough: The Classic Book on Improving Management Performance.* rev. ed. New York, NY: McGraw-Hill Professional, 1994.

Katzenbach, Jon R., and Doug K. Smith. *The Discipline of Teams: A Mindbook-Workbook for Delivering Small Group Performance.* New York, NY: John Wiley & Sons, Inc., 2001.

Klinvex, Kevin, Matthew O'Connell, and Christopher Klinvex. *Hiring Great People.* New York, NY: McGraw-Hill Professional, 1998.

Langdon, Ken, and Christine Osborne. *Essential Managers: Performance Reviews.* New York, NY: Dorling Kindersley Publishing, Inc., 2001.

Lencioni, Patrick. *The Five Temptations of a CEO: A Leadership Fable.* San Francisco, CA: Jossey-Bass Publishers, Inc., 1998.

Leonard, Dorothy, and Walter Swap. *When Sparks Fly: Igniting Creativity in Groups.* Boston, MA: Harvard Business School, 1999.

MacMillan, Pat. *The Performance Factor: Unlocking the Secrets of Teamwork.* Nashville, TN: Broadman & Holman Publishers, 2001.

Maguire, Francis X., and Steve Williford. *You're the Greatest: How Validated Employees Can Impact Your Bottom Line.* Germantown, TN: Williford Communications, 2001.

Maxwell, John C. *The 21 Irrefutable Laws of Leadership: Follow Them and People Will Follow You.* Nashville, TN: Thomas Nelson, 1998.

Maxwell, John C. *The 17 Indisputable Laws of Teamwork: Embrace Them and Empower Your Team.* Nashville, TN: Thomas Nelson, 2001.

Michaels, Ed, Helen Handfield-Jones, and Beth Axelrod. *The War for Talent.* Boston, MA: Harvard Business School, 2001.

Murray, Margo. *Beyond the Myths and Magic of Mentoring: How to Facilitate an Effective Mentoring Process*, rev. ed. San Francisco, CA: Jossey-Bass Publishers, Inc., 2001.

Napier, Rod, Patrick Sanaghan, Clint Sidle, and Patrick Saraghan. *High Impact Tools and Activities for Strategic Planning: Creative Techniques for Facilitating Your Organization's Planning Process.* New York, NY: McGraw-Hill Professional, 1997.

Nash, Sue. *Turning Team Performance Inside Out: Team Types and Temperament for High Impact Results.* Palo Alto, CA: Davies-Black Publishing, 1999.

Regan, Michael D. *The Journey to Teams: The New Approach to Achieve Breakthrough Business Performance.* Chelan, WA: Holden Press, 1999.

Rinke, Wolf J. *Winning Management: 6 Fail-Safe Strategies for Building High Performance Organizations.* Clarksville, MD: Achievement Publishers, 1997.

Schmidt, Warren H., B. J. Gallagher Hateley, and Sam Weiss. *Is It Always Right to Be Right?: A Tale of Transforming Workplace Conflict into Creativity and Collaboration.* New York, NY: AMACOM, 2001.

Searles, George J. *Workplace Communications: The Basics.* Boston, MA: Allyn & Bacon, Inc., 1999.

Senge, Peter M. *The Fifth Discipline: The Art and Practice of the Learning Organization.* Garden City, NJ: Doubleday & Company Inc., 1990.

Sims, Doris M. *Creative New Employee Orientation Programs: Best Practices, Creative Ideas, and Activities for Energizing Your Orientation Program.* New York, NY: McGraw-Hill Professional, 2001.

Smart, Bradford D. *Topgrading: How Leading Companies Win By Hiring, Coaching and Keeping the Best People.* Paramus, NJ: Prentice-Hall Press, 1999.

Spitzer, Dean R. *Supermotivation: A Blueprint for Energizing Your Organization from Top to Bottom.* New York, NY: AMACOM, 1995.

Still, Del J. *High Impact Hiring: How to Interview and Select Outstanding Employees.* Dana Point, CA: Management Development Systems, 1997.

Thomas, Kenneth W. *Intrinsic Motivation at Work: Building Energy and Commitment.* San Francisco, CA: Berrett-Koehler Publishers, 2000.

Tulgan, Bruce. *Winning the Talent Wars: How to Build a Lean, Flexible, High-Performance Workplace.* New York, NY: W. W. Norton & Company, Inc., 2002.

Whitworth, Laura, Henry Kimsey-House, and Phil Sandahl. *Co-Active Coaching: New Skills for Coaching People Toward Success in Work and Life.* Palo Alto, CA: Davies-Black Publishing, 1998.

Yate, Martin. *Hiring the Best: A Manager's Guide to Effective Interviewing*, 4th ed. Holbrook, MA: Adams Media, 1997.

Zemke, Ron, and Kristin Anderson. *Coaching Knock Your Socks Off Service*. New York, NY: AMACOM, 1996.

INDEX